EMPATH HEALING FOR BEGINNERS

2 Books in 1: Survival Guide for Highly Sensitive People. Improve Your Empathy Skills, Overcome Fear, Increase Self-Esteem, and Develop Emotional Intelligence

Valery Blake

© Copyright 2020 by Valery Blake. All right reserved.

The work contained herein has been produced with the intent to provide relevant knowledge and information on the topic on the topic described in the title for entertainment purposes only. While the author has gone to every extent to furnish up to date and true information, no claims can be made as to its accuracy or validity as the author has made no claims to be an expert on this topic. Notwithstanding, the reader is asked to do their own research and consult any subject matter experts they deem necessary to ensure the quality and accuracy of the material presented herein.

This statement is legally binding as deemed by the Committee of Publishers Association and the American Bar Association for the territory of the United States. Other jurisdictions may apply their own legal statutes. Any reproduction, transmission or copying of this material contained in this work without the express written consent of the copyright holder shall be deemed as a copyright violation as per the current legislation in force on the date of publishing and subsequent time thereafter. All additional works derived from this material may be claimed by the holder of this copyright.

The data, depictions, events, descriptions and all other information forthwith are considered to be true, fair and accurate unless the work is expressly described as a work of fiction. Regardless of the nature of this work, the Publisher is exempt from any responsibility of actions taken by the reader in conjunction with this work. The Publisher acknowledges that the reader acts of their own accord and releases the author and Publisher of any responsibility for the observance of tips, advice, counsel, strategies and techniques that may be offered in this volume.

TABLE OF CONTENTS

EMPATH FOR BEGINNERS
Improve Self-Esteem, Overcome Fear, Find Your Sense Of Self, Learn To Stop Absorbing Negative Energies, Increase Self-Confidence, Achieve Emotional Healing

Introduction 3
Chapter 1 *Understanding The Enigma Called An Empath* 6
Chapter 2 *It Is Not A Disease, Curse, Or A Problem* 11
Chapter 3 *It Is A Gift, But You Will Need To Learn A Lot To Harness It* 16
Chapter 4 *Possible Explanations Of Development Of Powers That Make You An Empath* 23
Chapter 5 *There Is A Difference Between Empathy And An Empath* 26
Chapter 6 *Who Is An Empath?* 30
Chapter 7 *The Struggles Of Living As An Unawakened Empath* 33
Chapter 8 *Unraveling The Nature Of An Empath* 37
Chapter 9 *What Does It Mean To Be An Empath?* 44
Chapter 10 *Do You Think You Are An Empath?* 53
Chapter 11 *All Empaths Aren't The Same- What Kind Of An Empath Are You?* 64
Chapter 12 *What Difference Does Being An Empath Have On Life?* 70
Chapter 13 72
The Thin Line Of Being An Empath 72
Chapter 14 *Beware Of The Things That Can Take You Down* 73
Chapter 15 *Learning To Be An Empath With Confidence* 78
Conclusion 81
Description 82

EMPATH HEALING
Beginner's Guide to Improve Your Empathy Skills, Increase Self-Esteem, Protect Yourself From Energy Vampires, and Overcome Fears With Emotional Intelligence

Introduction 86
Chapter 1 *Empath Healing- Why Is It Needed?* 87
Chapter 2 *What Does It Mean To Be An Empath?* 94
Chapter 3 *The Evolutionary Journey Of An Empath* 98
Chapter 4 *Being An Empath Can Be A Roller Coaster Ride* 102

Chapter 5 *Empaths And Emotions- Things To Heal Emotional Triggers* 104

Chapter 6 *Empaths And Addictions- The Why And How Of Getting Out Of It* 118

Chapter 7 *Empaths And Stress- Battling Sleeplessness And Fatigue* 124

Chapter 8 *Empaths And Relationships: Learning To Strike A Balance* 129

Chapter 9 *It Is Common For Empaths To Feel Exhausted-Understand The Signs That Your Soul Needs Healing*.. 138

Chapter 10: Self-Care Tips for Healing Exhaustion 141

Chapter 11 *Preventing Influence Of Negative Energies* 144

Chapter 12 *Energy Cleansing*..147

Chapter 13 Grounding Techniques for Empaths 151

Chapter 14 *Guided Meditations For Empaths* 156

Conclusion 165

Description.. 166

EMPATH FOR BEGINNERS

Improve Self-Esteem, Overcome Fear, Find Your Sense Of Self, Learn To Stop Absorbing Negative Energies, Increase Self-Confidence, Achieve Emotional Healing

Valery Blake

© Copyright 2020 by Valery Blake. All right reserved.

The work contained herein has been produced with the intent to provide relevant knowledge and information on the topic on the topic described in the title for entertainment purposes only. While the author has gone to every extent to furnish up to date and true information, no claims can be made as to its accuracy or validity as the author has made no claims to be an expert on this topic. Notwithstanding, the reader is asked to do their own research and consult any subject matter experts they deem necessary to ensure the quality and accuracy of the material presented herein.

This statement is legally binding as deemed by the Committee of Publishers Association and the American Bar Association for the territory of the United States. Other jurisdictions may apply their own legal statutes. Any reproduction, transmission or copying of this material contained in this work without the express written consent of the copyright holder shall be deemed as a copyright violation as per the current legislation in force on the date of publishing and subsequent time thereafter. All additional works derived from this material may be claimed by the holder of this copyright.

The data, depictions, events, descriptions and all other information forthwith are considered to be true, fair and accurate unless the work is expressly described as a work of fiction. Regardless of the nature of this work, the Publisher is exempt from any responsibility of actions taken by the reader in conjunction with this work. The Publisher acknowledges that the reader acts of their own accord and releases the author and Publisher of any responsibility for the observance of tips, advice, counsel, strategies and techniques that may be offered in this volume.

INTRODUCTION

Being an empath can be an overwhelming experience. An empath can be living a miserable life feeling the pain and agony without having any knowledge of it in real life. It usually makes things very complicated and challenging for the empath. Yet, openly talking about it or an attempt to explain it to others often results in ridicule. It can only mean one thing; in most cases than not, an empath is forced to live with the circumstances without a way out.

This book will help you in understanding the core issues and also the possible ways to deal with them. I congratulate you on purchasing this book, and thank you for doing so. In this book, I will try to explain what it means to be an empath and what an empath usually feels and goes through.

This book will try to help you understand the primary challenges in front of empaths and effective ways to deal with them.

Being an empath is not a curse as most people believe, and also not some powerful boon that popular literature tries to project. An empath isn't some sort of a mutant. This book will help you understand the realistic aspect of being an empath and how to deal with it in real life.

We will dig deep and understand what it means to be an empath and the impact it can have on life. There is a lot of confusion surrounding empaths. This book will try to explain that in detail so that you have better clarity on the subject.

It will explain the things that negatively influence the lives of empaths and also the attributes that will help them grow stronger.

This book will dwell upon the subject and explain what it means and who needs healing.

It will explain ways to enhance your abilities and ward off negative influences.

This book will deal with the concept of empath healing and how it can work for you. It would help you in overcoming your anxieties and keeping negative influences away while you try to find joy in life.

This book will try to debunk the myths most beginners have about empath healing and will set a clear and defined path so that you can develop a clear understanding of the subject.

This book is straightforward and easy to understand so that everyone can take advantage of this information.

I hope that you will be able to get the full advantage of this book.

There are plenty of books on this subject on the market; thanks again for choosing this one! Every effort has been made to ensure it is full of as much useful information as possible; please enjoy it!

PART I
BEING AN EMPATH

CHAPTER 1
Understanding The Enigma Called An Empath

Being an Empath is Normal

Our world has a high affinity for things being normal. It has rigid notions about all things being rational and standard, and anything that doesn't conform to those standards is abnormal.

- On meeting others, it is a norm to strike a conversation. People not trying to do that can be termed as abnormal or socially awkward.
- Our kind has always felt more secure in groups. People feeling insecure or uncomfortable in groups can also be termed as abnormal or awkward.
- We like to be in crowds, pretend to enjoy the company of others, but hide our genuine emotions or current emotional state. Yet strangely, if someone can sense those emotions or feels them, we begin feeling threatened or vulnerable. We may also call such a person abnormal.

Abnormal is a term the world has devised to brand anything that is beyond the average reach or common comprehension. It is the bracket in which empaths generally fall.

Being an empath is not abnormal. An empath is also like being any other person in the world. It is just that an empath has some additional powers than others, and sometimes even that individual fails to understand and appreciate those powers and abilities.

Who Is an Empath?

You are an empath if you have the superhuman ability to understand and absorb the mental or emotional state of others near you. Here, you would need to follow caution in comprehending the term carefully. Most people may be able to make an informed guess about someone else's mental or emotional state. Some people may even be able to address them emphatically. However, very few people with a special gift of deep sensitivity will be able to feel that mental or emotional state within themselves. Such people are empaths. Such people not only understand the pain others are feeling but also sense that pain deep within themselves.

A person can learn to be emphatic so that he/she can have better connections with others. An empath will be born with the sensitivities that help him/her in feeling the pain, emotions, and discomfort felt or experienced by others.

Being an empath can be a roller-coaster ride. An empath will feel people around, and their emotions will have a profound impact on him/her. These can be overwhelming experiences for an empath, and they can make an empath naturally shy of crowds or public exposure. An empath with poor control over the gift may find it increasingly challenging to be in large groups as the energies around the empath will be affecting him/her continuously, even without talking to the people with such powers.

Empaths are highly sensitive people. They can feel pain, emotions, energies of people around them far more intensely. However, the problem doesn't end just there. Some empaths with powerful sensitivities, and very porous boundaries can not only feel them but also begin absorbing them. It can become a challenge as they become a storehouse of all the negative energy, pain, and stress around them.

Hence, an empath can be an individual with a superhuman ability to look deep inside the heart and mind of a person in front beyond the surface level façade. Such empaths can play a significant role in helping others as they are gifted healers.

However, an empath can also be a person who is unable to control the amount of negative energy seeping in and hence forced to live in constant pain and discomfort.

These are just the two sides of being an empath. On the contrary to what most people think, being an empath is neither a curse nor a boon; it is merely a state of heightened sensitivities and the amount of command and understanding an individual has over them.

Some empaths may have comparatively low sensitivities and may not get affected too much. Whereas others can have relatively much higher sensitivities, and they may keep feeling overwhelmed most of the time if they have not strengthened personal boundaries.

Irrespective of the level of sensitivities you have, being an empath is not a curse. If you have not yet mastered control over your sensibilities, you may feel overwhelmed with negative energies, thoughts, and feelings. It isn't even very uncommon to have a strong aversion to crowded places. It is all very much possible and common. However, this is not how it has to be forever.

An empath can quickly learn to use this gift of heightened sensitivities to read people around and have a deep insight into the human psyche.

Some of the most potent characteristics that may make the life of an empath difficult. However, an empath can easily handle it if he/she learns to manage the powers properly.

An empath is neither a maniac nor a wizard. An empath is also just like everyone else, a great human being with some gifts that the empath can sharpen and use as tools for healing others. However, if the empath chooses to ignore them, they can turn into thorns that may start creating a lot of nuisance within.

Boons and Banes of an Empath

Character traits of an empath can be many, and I have not taken the best of those here because most empaths may not have all of them in common. These are the four traits that are usually common in most empaths and need to be understood carefully, or else they can turn even against them.

Intuitive

It is the most common and most understandable trait in empaths. Everyone has some degree of intuition. The gut feeling within us warns us of dangers and guides us away from them. This feeling is the best answer in most circumstances for us. However, empaths have a special gift of intuition. They are highly sensitive beings with the ability to listen to their inner thoughts when it comes to judging others carefully. It is effortless for them to distinguish between positive and negative energies in others as they can feel them directly.

The events in the future are a direct result of the actions in the present, and the intuitiveness of any individual can help in determining it. Because empaths have a clear edge in this area, they are better at guessing future events.

However, even this outstanding power can work against empaths if they do not exercise proper control of their capabilities and emotions. Empaths are highly sensitive beings, and they can quickly get motivated to cut themselves off from others to block the inflow of negative energies that can help them in being intuitive.

Some empaths may also begin relying on other inputs like their dreams, telepathic contributions, precognitive abilities, and sensations around them, and this can also increase their intuitive powers.

All these are powers that empaths can utilize if they have realized their gift. Not all empaths will be able to recognize all the abilities, and some may not be able to achieve any of these, yet they have a world of opportunities open in front of them to utilize.

Realizing the power of intuition comes quickly to an empath because the sensitivities are very high. However, it is a gift that needs to be harnessed through practice and focus on gut feelings. It is also the gift that will help an empath in forging strong relationships.

Most empaths are vulnerable to energy vampires that can drain them of all the emotional energy and leave them feeling exhausted. The toxic behavior of people around you can begin stressing them physically, mentally, and emotionally.

The power of intuition can help an empath in avoiding such people and situations. However, all empaths may not have the power of intuition developed in the same manner. But, empaths can augment this power nonetheless, and being an empath always helps.

Intense

Being an empath doesn't come without some riders, and being intense is one among them. An empath is an individual who feels things far more strongly than others. It means that something that may not even lead to a passing thought in the mind of a person may shake an empath deeply. For instance, we oversee many unfortunate people and beings while passing on a road. Most people don't even bat an eyelid as they are busy with their lives. However, that may not turn out to be the case with an empath. An empath may feel deeply saddened by the sight or mere presence of such people around. If helping such people is not possible, the pain and hurt may stay deep inside the heart of an empath.

In the same way, an empath may also feel other emotions like love and trust profoundly and may get hurt more thoroughly than others.

Uncentered

It is another battle that an empath may have to fight all life. An empath may not be able to feel at home most of the time. There is always a feeling somewhere at the back of the mind that something is out of place or something isn't right.

This anxiety comes out of the perpetual outside energy influence an empath keeps getting that leaves that unsettling feeling.

It is not a quality or gift or even a curse; it is just a trait that empaths usually exhibit.

Perplexed

For an unawakened empath, it is not uncommon to feel perplexed most of the time. Empaths have to live in the constant agony of feeling everything wanted or unwanted around them. They experience the emotions of others around them and remain filled with pain and anguish. They have weak personal boundaries, and hence separating feelings of others, and the self keeps on becoming increasingly difficult for them. Either it is the painful exposure to large crowds or the guilty pleasure of having seclusion, unawakened empaths have a hard time either way. A struggle between pain and guilt is always going on.

However, that's not an experience for every empath. An awakened empath knows the art of regulating their emotions. They have firm personal boundaries that allow them to experience the feelings of others without getting lost in them.

An awakened empath would know the art of not getting lost in the problem while trying to solve it. It isn't an ability that one is born with by default. It is something that an empath needs to learn and practice.

Usually, people have absurd ideas about empaths. Most of their knowledge comes from exaggerated fiction portrayed on the idiot box and leisure literature.

Empaths are not a distinct breed or mutants with some elaborate powers. A very high number of individuals are born with above-average sensitivity. They feel emotions with higher intensity than others.

It is a fact that empaths have a heightened sense of perception and intuition, but that doesn't make them fortune-tellers. Every coin has two sides, and being an empath is no exception.

An unawakened empath with weak boundaries may live a life of suffering and pain. There is no respite for such empaths as they may feel lost all the time. Their power of discernment between their own emotions and emotions perceived by others may become weak. They may not have any respite from the constant bombardment of emotions that they do not understand, and it will take a toll on their emotional, mental, as well as physical health.

Therefore, contrary to popular beliefs, being an empath is not a bed of roses. It is just a weak and troubled mental and emotional state for the empath.

However, all that can change for an awakened empath who has control over his/her senses. A confident and awakened empath may not have the ability to predict the future or read the minds of people around him. Still, they will have the ability to assess people correctly based on the first impression left by them.

A well-functioning empath will also have the power of intuition and hence would have a better grip over things.

Therefore, being an empath is neither a bed of roses or a spikey seat. It is an ability with which you are born. It isn't something that'd go with time, and hence ignoring it won't help. If you keep forgetting it for long enough, it may fill you with anxiety, distrust, anguish, pain, and disharmony. However, if you work upon your gift, you may not only be able to get hold of your senses but also help others around you.

This book would help you in understanding what an empath means and the way to carry out empath healing so that one can stay on the right path.

CHAPTER 2
It Is Not A Disease, Curse, Or A Problem

Being an Empath- Boon or Bane?

It is not uncommon for humankind, in general, to fear and blame things, it has difficulty in understanding. Empaths need not be an exception. Even as a child, when an individual begins to show traits of an empath like:-
- Overly sensitive or shy nature
- Frequent bouts of anxiety or getting overwhelmed
- Inability to tolerate shouting or arguments
- Anxiety in crowds
- Inability to correctly fit in the mix
- Desire to remain socially isolated
- A tendency to absorb pain, stress, emotions, and symptoms of other people around

But, an Empath
- Finds it easy to assess the nature of others
- Has accurate gut feeling most of the time
- Begins predicting many events, yet to occur, with accuracy
- Develops a unique and more accurate understanding of people
- Feels the pain and sorrow of others in a real sense and can heal them better

It is common for people, including even that individual, to look for faults and problems.

As an empath, a person may:

Experience Increased Sensitivity to Light, Sound, Smell, Taste, Touch, and Temperature: This is among the first experiences an empath may have. Even as a newborn, empaths may exhibit high sensitivity to bright lights, loud noises, exotic smells, and other sensory stimuli. Such stimuli can be painful, startling, frightening, or shocking. Not only that, but it also isn't necessary for two empaths to get agitated by the same stimuli.

Begin Absorbing Stress, Emotions, and Negativity of Others: This is a common trait of empaths. They can begin absorbing the stress, emotions, and negative energies emitted by people around them. Unawakened empaths have no barriers, and hence they can't control what they consume. They are very porous, and anything and everything around them begins affecting them.

Prone to Stimulation: Empaths can begin feeling overstimulated quickly. The things that may not stimulate ordinary people easily, an empath may feel highly agitated. They may start feeling exhausted and need more alone time to replenish their energy.

Feel Things More Intensely Than Others: Empaths are sensitive. They get affected by visuals and emotions that aren't even happening in real-time. For instance, if they are only watching something graphic full of violence or sorrow, they can feel the same within themselves. They don't have filters to keep such emotions out.

Experience Emotional Burnout: They are always ready to listen to others. If the stories they hear have emotions, grief, and pain, they begin affecting them with the same intensity. It can also start causing overexertion. Every empath needs to learn to build boundaries and respect them, which most don't, becoming the cause of the trouble.

Feel Lonely and Isolated: Being an empath is maintaining a tricky balance. You open up a tad bit more, and you'll expose your boundaries and begin getting bombarded by emotions, you tighten the latch, and you'd become private. The need to have some respite usually wins, and people tend to prefer more and more seclusion leading to loneliness and social isolation. The real trick is to open up the gates but to enforce more definite boundaries, and then only an empath can have a social presence along with the peace of mind.

As you can imagine, most empaths struggle all their lives to find that balance or peace of mind because the personal space of an empath keeps getting bombarded by emotions.

Suffering and pain become part and parcel of an empath's life and finds it difficult to come to terms with the reality of creating boundaries and personal space.

Loneliness, depression, pain, overwhelming emotions, emotional confusion, and distress become a regular feature in the life of such empaths. They keep getting dragged by these and find it very hard to carry the burden of all these things.

Having a heightened sense of perceptions, intuition, and precognition can begin looking like a curse if you do not have an understanding of your gifts or know the art to utilize them. **Imagine a bird having acrophobia *(Fear of Height)*.**

Have you heard of the 'Midas Touch'? Midas had the power to turn anything into gold by a simple touch. It was a boon. Yet, it became a bane because it starved him. Even the food touched by him turned into gold.

Empaths have a heightened perception of pain, suffering, and emotions of others. As long as they can enforce boundaries around them to prevent illness, suffering, and feelings of others from permeating into them, they will be able to help others and live a fruitful life. The problem begins when empaths fail to have such boundaries, and they start acting like a blotting paper soaking up all the pain and suffering around them.

Being an empath is not a problem. The inability to have sufficient control over your power, condition, or traits is the cause of the malice that empaths face.

Being an empath is not a disease, a curse, or a problem.

It is a gift you need to encash. Recognizing and realizing this gift is a must. Once you recognize this gift, you'll know the number of lives you can touch with your abilities.

There Can Be Challenges, But You Aren't Crazy

In the beginning, unawakened empaths fail to understand that the confusion, delusion, and a series of emotions unrelated to their personal experiences are just a part of being an empath.

All empaths are highly sensitive people. It merely means that they can feel the emotions and energies around them more profoundly than others. Not only the powers of people around them, but some may also be able to handle the vibrancy radiated from the plants and animals.

Generally, unawakened empaths aren't able to differentiate between the emotions originating within them and the pain, suffering, and emotions absorbed from the environment, and this can leave them perplexed. The thought that they might be crazy or abnormal may easily cross their mind several times.

The higher the number of recurrences of such instances, the more cemented the belief that they might be crazy gets.

Biggest Misconception to Be Cleared

The mental troubles, emotional burdens, unhappiness, and delusions are not because they are empaths. It is there because they haven't done anything to strengthen their defenses. Unawakened empaths are usually porous, and hence there is nothing to stop the feelings and emotions of others from affecting them.

Being an empath makes you capable in one direction. You get an advantage in something. However, every new power comes with a cost. Being an empath makes you capable of feeling emotions and energies with higher sensitivity that others can't. But that comes with a price. You open up to a whole lot of emotions and energies around you.

You'd need to learn to be selective. You can't let this be overused.

Consider your hypersensitivities to be a battery-operated accessory. If you keep it powered on all the time, even though it may not be performing any useful function, it'd be using up the battery. Because the accessory would be on and geared up, it'd also keep getting entangled here and there, adding to the trouble.

Therefore, you'll see that keeping it powered on all the time is not only inefficient and energy-draining but also an added pain.

The same is the case with empaths and the extra-sensory powers they possess.

An empath can have hypersensitivities in a wide range of areas. An empath may also attract negative energies and have weak boundaries. Getting influenced by them would become easy. You will have very little control over them.

These will keep posing challenges in front of an empath. The important thing is to realize that you aren't crazy, and there is a way to get control of the situation, and it isn't challenging.

Public Ridicule, Unanswered Questions, and Constant Tussles Can be Addressed

Public Ridicule

It can be challenging for the uninitiated to understand the qualities an empath may possess. It may lead to public ridicule. However, public ridicule over your abilities, sensitivities, and behavior must be your last concern as society in general never understands people who don't fall in their standard. It has always ridiculed, mocked, and outcast people it didn't understand. Most renowned scientists, reformers, and harbingers of social change have had to face that, and hence that is something that must not concern you.

When the society ridicules, it merely means either you are doing something wrong that doesn't conform to its standards, or you are doing something it doesn't understand. As long as you aren't doing something illegal, you do not need to worry.

Unanswered Questions

It is natural for an empath to have a lot of unanswered questions. There can be a lot that an empath may not understand. There are no exact answers to 'why,' but there are answers to 'what now.'

An empath may have a lot of questions.

- Why do they feel the way they do?
- Why do they feel so drained in the company of others?
- Why is their power of intuition better than others?
- Why do they feel so overwhelmed in public places?
- Why are they so emotional?
- Why are they always so inclined to help others?
- Why is it so hard for them to say no and avoid toxic people?
- Why do they even feel emotions utterly unrelated to their experiences?
- What is the reason for scattered thoughts and the mind-fog they experience?

These are just some of the questions. The list can be endless, as every empath can have completely different struggles and experiences.

However, the answer to all the mental clutter lies in understanding your abilities and reinforcing your boundaries.

Empaths are prone to get influenced by the external energies as they are very porous. But, that doesn't always have to be the case always. You can still learn to strengthen personal defenses and only allow emotions and energies with the private sphere selectively. It is possible to master it, and you can easily do it with practice.

Constant Tussles

An empath may feel constant trouble all the time as the mind and heart may not agree on the same things. There will be times when your intuition will be telling you to do something while common sense may be directing you in a completely different direction. All this is not only possible but also highly probable.

Most empaths have an intuitive power that's reliable, and that may make them sense danger or sticky situations even when it isn't visible through logic. Also, most of the time, empaths will be able to form a very accurate description of a person meeting for the first time based on the first impression. It is besides the fact that most people try to hide their true nature in the first meeting and seek to be at their best behavior. However, hiding true self from empaths can be difficult as they can sense the energies and vibes more accurately.

However, gut feelings and vibes do not conform to popular logic, and this may lead to constant tussles. They may find it hard to determine what to do and what to put aside.

You must understand that these are minor struggles that an empath undergoes. An empath can easily overcome these struggles by following the gift and learning to harness that gift.

An awakened empath will be in a much better position to use the powers effectively and conduct life without dilemmas. The answers to complicated questions would come quickly, and without a doubt and trusting the gut feeling would become much more comfortable for an empath.

It is essential that you clearly understand that being an empath is not a disease or a curse. It is an unrealized boon. You can learn to harness this energy to lead a perfectly balanced life and also have some additional powers to help others whom no one understands.

CHAPTER 3
It Is A Gift, But You Will Need To Learn A Lot To Harness It

Discovering and Appreciating the Gift and Seeking Answers

Being an empath is not a choice we make. It is something most empaths are born with or develop these sensitivities in exceptional circumstances like accidents, violent encounters, and other such traumatic events.

Initially, it can be reasonable to be confused about the powers and various sensations that may come along, as all of them may be unpleasant. However, it is prudent to adapt to the changes you are experiencing and discover your gift.

Living with these powers is like getting trapped in a room with a ferocious dog. Either you'll learn to tame that dog and make it act upon your instructions, or that dog will make your life difficult with constant growling, threatening, and attacks.

The realization of your powers is the first step towards real emancipation. You must realize that these are powers, and they can help you in helping others as well as yourself.

An empath is a person who can feel the pain and emotions of others more deeply. However, just sensing the problem is not going to help anyone. It is only going to propagate that pain at one other place, i.e., in your heart. If you realize your gift, you'll be able to address the issue specifically and help yourself and others.

Doing that is not very difficult, contrary to what most people believe. It is a gift that's inside you, and you only need to realize it. Some simple efforts can help you in achieving your abilities quickly and make you feel that being an empath is not a bane but a boon.

However, that's not going to happen until you acknowledge, accept, and appreciate your gift.

If you want to own your gift in the real sense, you must:

Acknowledge the Gift: If you are an empath, feeling for others will be your second nature. The harder you try to fight it, the more difficult it'll get for you. It is a gift that you possess, and you must acknowledge and appreciate it.

There will be times when people would find it easy to overlook someone in distress and pretend as if nothing is happening. There is no need for you to imitate as if you also belong in that group.

As an empath, feeling the pain of others would be your second nature. You'd be able to sense a lot of things that others won't, and there is no need to be embarrassed about them. There is no measure for that.

You must acknowledge that you feel that you feel differently than others. Your senses are more durable and more powerful. You may not only be able to feel the pain and emotion visible in front but may also be able to handle the energies around you.

Do Not Undermine Your Gut Feeling: Our gut feeling is an exceptional phenomenon. It can help us make strange decisions. Most people have a gut feeling fuelled by the stress hormones and lead to a fight or flight response. For them, the gut feeling is just an escape mechanism devised just to escape uncomfortable scenarios.

However, gut feeling or intuition can be a very distinct phenomenon for empaths. They have very high sensitivities, and their instinct is mostly a sum of those sensitivities. As an empath, if you are sensing danger at someplace, it is better to trust your gut feeling than to take chances as the likeliness of your intuition turning out to be true is very high.

While intuition is an escape mechanism in most people, for an empath, it can be a survival mechanism.

Setting Boundaries: Weak personal boundaries are among the most significant cause of concern for empaths. You can term empaths to be friendly people who can get affected by the pain of others. They do not need the spoken word for feeling the pain of others. They may act as magnets for such pain and suffering. Their energy fields are constantly scanning for people in pain and may be able to feel the pain of others in the vicinity. It can be a big challenge, and there is no way a person will be able to help all, and hence the life of an empath can become an unending saga of pain.

It is not unnatural for people to recognize such empaths and then begin exploiting the weakness about helping others. Such clingy people can also become energy vampires that may become very demanding and draining. The only way out of this problem is to have firm personal boundaries. Empaths would have to train themselves to recognize such energy vampires. It is something that may take time, but they'll be able to identify those people that are a constant energy drain.

They'll also have to strengthen their energy fields so that they do not keep getting bombarded with unsolicited emotions. They'll have to learn the art of managing their energy field more strongly.

Learn to Push Away Negative Energy: It is easier said than done to propel negative energy and influences. Most people feel the vibes and energy fields emitted by others. Even in your first meeting, most people can form liking or dislike about anyone, and most likely, it stays with them. It is also true for everyone in general. Now think of an empath who has a distinct ability to feel the energy vibes far more intensely.

They will be able to feel the vibes and would keep reacting to them latently, and that would also cause a lot of energy drain. It can become a big problem if there are such toxic people at the work-place or in the neighborhood. That can make the life of an empath very difficult. The easy way out for an empath is to learn to find ways to absorb or push away negative energies. There are several natural energy modulators like crystals, beautiful artifacts, and plants that can help in absorbing negative energies around you, and you'll be able to work far more peacefully.

Shun the Feeling of Victimhood: The need for love, admiration, and adoration is always there in most of us. It is natural for someone with intense feelings to have these needs even more. The fact that they feel more strongly for others and can feel the emotions better makes them long even more for the love and devotion of others.

However, empaths are complicated. They are not superficial. It can be challenging for others to understand them and have a fine-tuning with them, and this can leave them longing for love, admiration, and appreciation.

An empath may have to learn to find love differently without losing self-worth in front of others. Realization of true self-worth is essential for empaths without being proud or boastful about it if they want to find true love and objective in their lives.

Learn to love Yourself: This is one of the most critical lessons for an empath. You must learn to love yourself. There should be no room for self-pity. You must understand that until you love and learn to appreciate yourself, your energy fields would remain weak, and you'll keep feeling vulnerable.

You Must Learn to Take Out Exhaustion and Bring Relief

It is a fact that you'll realize very soon. Empaths may begin feeling exhausted very soon. It is natural for them to feel so. Allowing so many emotions to pass over you and maintaining composure can be very taxing.

Therefore,

An Empath Must Set a Regular Sleep-Wake Cycle

Being an empath can be an everyday struggle. It isn't something that you can stop doing. An empath can begin feeling overwhelmed even by watching something on the TV or a news item. Hence, avoiding such stimuli or cutting yourself from the outside world to relax is not a practical solution.

Most people talk of a digital detox these days as there is very high information overload taking place from digital media, and escaping it is next to impossible. We are on the internet for our work, needs, and leisure all the time. It means our exposure to information coming from the internet is also very high.

Knowingly or unknowingly, this information keeps piling up and has an impact on our overall functioning ability. Typically, people can function with it, but things can be stressful with an empath as information gets processed differently in their minds. They are far more sensitive, and it may weigh them down.

Empaths must set a regular sleep-wake cycle to maintain high functionality so that their body and mind can get the needed rest.

Take Regular Breaks

Nothing can be more refreshing than regular breaks for an empath. Empaths experience emotions, feelings, and grief more intensely. Either it is a meeting or any work, they remain immersed with complete attention, and that can become very taxing.

Regular breaks can help an empath in re-energizing himself/herself and work better.

These breaks don't need to be longer, but they need to be more frequent. Even a little bit of distraction from the intense environment can help an empath in winding down and regaining the energy to function optimally. Therefore, you must keep taking short breaks as often as possible.

Deep-Breathing Exercise

It is the most important advice of the three. Deep breathing is the best tool an empath has to gather awareness and focus.

It is usual for an empath to keep getting bombarded with emotions, feelings, grief, joy, and a plethora of such emotions. They can be disturbing and distracting. They may take away focus from the main objective or even cause disorientation.

It is also easy for an empath to begin feeling agitated, flushed, sad, and disoriented. Managing all these emotions when they come without proper context can be difficult. The best way to manage them is to practice deep breathing.

Deep breathing is a simple practice that can help an empath gather awareness and bring it back to reality.

The human mind is very volatile and gets distracted easily. It can begin producing thoughts that can be even more distracting and disorienting. The best way to deal with such situations and to keep them at bay is to breathe deeply.

Whenever you begin feeling agitated or have thoughts that are causing distraction or discomfort, you can do the following:

If, it is possible, find a place to sit down comfortably
If you are standing, find a place to support your body
Keep your spine erect
Please keep your neck straight
Your shoulders should be straight but not stiff
Now, if possible, please close your eyes
For a minute, feel the silence
Please try to gather all your thoughts

There is no need to control anything
Don't try to control your thoughts
Don't try to control your breathing
Simply, become aware of your thoughts
(Pause)
Imagine it is a peaceful time now
Even a minute of silence can be of great help
Now, please bring your awareness to your breathing
Simply observe your breathing process with your awareness
No need to control your breathing yet
There is no need to do anything
Just try to become aware of your surrounding
Try to feel with all your senses
Try to hear the faintest noises in your surrounding
Please focus on any kind of noise you can hear
Even if noise is coming from the fan or the air conditioning in the room
Try to notice any other noise in the surrounding
(Long pause)
Try to feel with your body
Observe the sensation of clothes touching your skin
The sensation air creates when it touches the skin
Any other kind of sensation that you might be able to feel
(Long pause)
Now, try to smell
Try to observe the fragrance in the air
Any kind of essence that you might feel
(Long pause)
With your eyes closed
Through your awareness
Silently observe the way you breathe
At this moment, you do not need to control your breathing
Jut observe the process of breathing
Breathe in
Breathe out
Breathe in
Breathe out
Breathe in
Breathe out
Your focus may waver
You may start getting thoughts
That's alright!
There is no need to bother
Simply bring your awareness back to the process of breathing
Breathe in
Breathe out

Breathe in
Breathe out
Breathe in
Breathe out
Now, we will practice deep breathing
In this process, we will slowly take deep breaths to the count of 5
Then, hold your breath to the count of 5
And, release the breath even slower to the count of 7
It will calm the mind and drive all the negative thoughts away
Through this whole process
Please keep your awareness focused on the process of breathing
If your consciousness wanders, simply bring it back
Now, very slowly and steadily start breathing in
1.....2.......3.........4............5
Very good!
Now, hold this breath
1.....2.......3.........4............5
Better!
Now, exhale even slower
1.....2.......3.........4............5..............6..................7
Excellent!
The process of deep breathing calms the mind
It takes away all the thoughts
The mind becomes focused on the most crucial activity for life
Breathing
Breathe in
Breathe out
Breathe in
Breathe out
Breathe in
Breathe out
Again,
Take a deep breath in through your nostrils
1... Draw your breath slowly
2..... There is no rush
3....... Feel the breath coming in
4. .... Observe the sensation it creates at the point of entry
5............. Try to feel whether the air is hot or cold
Now, hold this breath for a few seconds
1.... Let the air seep deep inside your body
2.......Let it oxygenate your blood
3.........You might feel some pressure
4...........Do not be alarmed, this pressure is good
5............. Let this air reach every cell in your body
Now, breathe out through your mouth

1.... Let the air go out slowly
2...... Do not rush
3.........Let all your worries and anxieties go out with this spent air
4............Clear your body of all the negative energy
5................ Make way for positivity
6..................Push out all the pessimism
7.......................Clear out all the air
Now, relax
Enjoy the relaxing experience of deep breathing
(Long Pause)
Breathe In
Breathe Out
Breathe In
Breathe Out
Breathe In
Breathe Out
Bring your awareness back to your surrounding
Without opening your eyes
Try to feel through all your senses
Keep breathing normally
Allow your breathing to become rhythmic
Now, you can gently open your eyes

Deep breathing is a very relaxing practice. You can perform it anywhere and make it as long or short as you want. The primary purpose of the in-depth breathing process is to bring all your senses back to you and focus them inwards and not outwards.

Deep breathing helps in bringing your wandering awareness back to you, and you'll be able to administer better control over your emotions and behavior.

If you are feeling overwhelmed or agitated, deep breathing can be immensely helpful, and it can make you feel relaxed.

CHAPTER 4
Possible Explanations Of Development Of Powers That Make You An Empath

An empath is an enigma. There is no clear explanation of why an empath must behave in the way he/she behaves. Most people believe it has something to do with our neurons, and our understanding of them is already minimal.

Others believe that the strong reception of emotions may be a result of some electromagnetic waves working vigorously in empaths. At the same time, some also think that it can be the work of some 'enthusiastic contagion.'

Several hypotheses try to explain the reason why some individuals can feel the emotions of others so strongly. However, all these are still hypotheses, and there is no actual knowledge about the exact cause.

It makes one thing clear, and that is the need to learn to live with it. There is no way you are going to be able to shake it off, and hence the faster you learn to live with it, the better.

Although an unawakened empath may feel overwhelmed, once a person learns to deal with this gift, things become comparatively easy. I have still used the expression relatively easy and not fantastic because you must not forget that an empath may have to go through a storm of emotions daily despite having all the control, command, and boundaries. Some feelings can be overwhelming even for the most experienced and awakened empaths.

However, every gift comes with some riders, and having to feel what others can't is the rider that comes with the advantage of being able to sense better than others.

Possible Scientific Explanations of the Way an Empath Feels

The Mirror Neuron System

Scientists have identified synapses that propagate empathy. It means that the people in whom those synapses are present in large numbers will be able to feel the pain experienced by others better than the ones who don't have them. These synapses act as reflective mirrors of the feelings of dread, torment, agony, and satisfaction.

Scientists believe that individuals that have a large number of such mirror neurons will be able to feel the pain, agony, and emotions of others deeply. Studies have also suggested that empaths have these mirror neurons in large quantities, and hence they are capable of more profound empathy.

Although the explanation is very close to being perfect, there is little explanation of the fact why empaths can feel emotions when they do not have direct exposure to them. It means that an empath can also begin feeling the pain and agony of a person who is nearby but not directly exposed to the empath.

Then there are several types of empaths with their distinct qualities, and explanation of all kinds is not present.

Although the mirror neuron theory only partially explains the transmitting of emotions from one person to another, it is still among the best explanations.

Electromagnetic Field

Some experts also believe that the heart and mind transmit electromagnetic waves that can lead to the spread of emotions and feelings from one person to an empath. It is a theory that fits the receiver-transmitter explanation in which everyone else is a transmitter, and the empath is a receiver. An empath can catch the bandwidth and feel those emotions.

Enthusiastic Contagion

It is another theory that tries to explain the phenomenon. It propagates an idea that states that most people release feelings of pain, excitement, joy, sorrow. The people around can catch these feelings at different levels and react accordingly.

Some people get affected by the virus of these feelings and begin reacting similarly, and that's why some news items genuinely fill a few individuals with excitement. In contrast, others may not respond that way.

It is like in a similar situation of panic; some people may begin to run and trample others while some may maintain calm and try to analyze the situation. It also doesn't explain the reason why people would give a similar reaction if they hear that news piece on the phone or they get to listen to it from other sources because, in that case, there would be no active reaction spread.

All these are theories that try to explain the phenomenon experienced by empaths. As you can see, science is still doing the guesswork, and that's why traditional medication is not very helpful in addressing the problems faced by empaths.

If an empath is suffering from excessive emotional overload or unable to control the surge of pain and emotions, the way out is through understanding the issue and finding practical solutions.

PART II
UNDERSTANDING WHAT IT MEANS TO BE AN EMPATH

CHAPTER 5
There Is A Difference Between Empathy And An Empath

The word 'empath' has a lot of mystical aura around it. The portrayal of empath characters in popular series has also not only given air to the mysticism but also popularized empaths a lot. Although this fame has drawn the attention of ordinary people towards empaths, sadly, there is also a lot of misinformation. Most of the information is beyond reality at best, making people think of empaths differently.

The simple truth is that empaths are neither magicians, mutants, not psychics. Empaths have special powers to feel energies and emotions around them more profoundly. You could sum the basics of the ability to that.

Accentuated Abilities

Some people are born with hawk eyes and can see much better than others. Others can listen better and more sharply. Some people are natural-born swimmers, while others are born runners. In the same way, while all of us have the power of intuition and the ability to sense energy and feel positive or negative vibes, some are born with the talent to detect them more intensely. Such people are called empaths.

Empaths are not abnormal people. They are also ordinary people with extraordinary power to sense the feelings of others deeply.

Peculiar Struggles

The struggles of empaths can be very different from others around them. Empaths not only feel the energies around them more profoundly, but they also act like sponges when it comes to feelings and emotions of others around them. Now, as you may know, this world is full of pain, suffering, and miseries. Absorbing feelings and emotions from the environment can quickly turn into a curse for an empath.

Most unawakened empaths who do not have substantial barriers around them or haven't trained themselves can keep absorbing such feelings and emotions, and this can make their lives very difficult. The simple act of watching TV or witnessing something painful that's not even happening in front of them in real-time can also fill them with grief. If you look around, you'll realize how difficult life can be for an empath in such circumstances.

The Difference Between Empathy and Empaths

Now, most people think that they can read and understand what others feel, and that doesn't sound that bad. The ability to understand what others are feeling and bringing yourself to that level of emotion is called empathy. It is an act of kindness. Your heart weeps for the pain suffered by others.

However, for an empath, it isn't a simple act of kindness but a natural and uncontrolled reaction. An empath will be able to feel that pain and suffering of the same intensity without having the backing of the experience bringing that reaction. Hence, most of the time, it can be confusing and complicated.

Empathy is a general human trait that makes us more humane. It helps us become kind and compassionate. However, most of the time, such compassion is superficial, and people can shrug off the feeling as soon as they leave the scene.

It isn't as simple and easy for empaths. The pain and emotions felt by them are of the same intensity, and they stay with empaths. Shrugging them off or mere pretending isn't possible for them.

Living like an empath isn't easy. An empath constantly gets bombarded by unsolicited emotions. One doesn't choose to be an empath. It gets passed on from one generation to another.

If an empath doesn't learn to cope with the emotions and works channelizing the energy properly, life can become increasingly confusing with time.

The Biggest Problem

The biggest problem that most empaths feel is that they are not able to differentiate whether the emotion they are feeling is their own or of someone else. The identification is missing, and that can make their lives miserable.

They always remain in a fix and are never able to determine the difference. It isn't just a problem for themselves but also a problem for others.

Suppose you get the power to feel the hunger of others and also have the capacity to feed. However, you are unable to identify whether it is you who is feeling hungry or someone else is hungry.

Every time that feeling of hunger strikes you, then chances are, you'll end up eating without the need of food. While this will make you overweight, others would still starve.

Weak identification can become a cause of the big problem, and it can quickly happen with empaths who don't realize their gift.

Most empaths never realize their gift and end up leading a miserable life. A power that could have enabled them to help others and heal them keeps making their lives difficult.

They'll not be able to enjoy life like others because crowded places would keep making them feel vulnerable. They'd keep feeling exhausted just by venturing out and may develop strong aversion from social gatherings and crowded places.

Many empaths may feel that their nature of getting overwhelmed anytime without provocation is a big problem. They may think that the lack of control is a nuisance, and they have no power to control it. However, that depends on the perspective of the empath and his/her preparation to deal with it.

Identification Is Important

The first step towards solving any problem is its identification. The way our society functions in general, most issues are easily brushed under the carpet. It is common for people to advise others with severe psychological problems to laugh it off or try to remain more engaged, and everything will get alright.

People categorize all obese people as voracious eaters and begin advising them to have control over their diet. They firmly believe that a lack of control over the desire to eat can be the only reason behind weight gain. They do not even consider factors like genetic makeup, comorbidities, depression, and other such factors.

It is a natural desire to overlook problems or undervalue them. However, shying away from the problem doesn't solve them. On the contrary, it can escalate it.

People know very little of empaths. The people who do not belong to the class of empaths but have comparatively higher sensitivities would like to have the title of being an empath. Popular fiction has created an air of mystery and power around empaths that makes the traits sound desirable. However, actual empaths are dealing with real problems. They have to struggle with emotions and sensitivities. They are not at the luxury of thinking about the fancy title of being an empath.

You must understand that being an empath is not a problem. But, not dealing with the issues that come along with it can be. Everyone who feels for the challenges of others isn't an empath. Understanding the problems of others is empathy, where you try to invoke the pain of others within yourself. There you try to imagine what others might be feeling. An empath is a person who feels that pain and emotions of others from within.

Some highly sensitive people might also be able to feel the pain and emotions of others. They are also very sensitive to light and sound. They have an aversion to large groups or crowded places. They may also have a deep desire to help others and would be able to feel their pain.

But empaths go even further than that. Empaths can also feel subtle energy. An empath may be able to experience the feelings and emotions of even those life forms that are unable to express themselves. An empath has the power to internalize the pain and emotions of others instantly. These are some distinguishing traits that only empaths have.

The world may always find it challenging to identify and understand an empath. But, an empath needs to have a correct assessment of the self. That is a must for the betterment of the empath as well as society.

CHAPTER 6
Who Is An Empath?

An empath is an ordinary individual with an open spirit. Defining all empaths in a single statement is impossible because empaths are of various kinds. However, the most common trait among all empaths is their high sensitivity. All empaths are highly sensitive individuals.

Empaths are individuals with the unique ability to feel subtle energy around them. These highly sensitive individuals can absorb the emotions, feelings, and pain of others around them. They act as sponges for feelings and emotions.

These are the qualities or traits common among empaths. But, it isn't an exhaustive list. Empaths can be of different kinds. Some empaths may easily absorb the physical symptoms of people around them, while others may act as sponges of emotions and feelings. Some empaths have intuitive abilities, while others may possess telepathic powers. From feeling the needs of the plants and vegetation around them to healing others, there are a lot of things that empaths can do.

However, before all this, an empath must have the realization of these powers and control over the vulnerabilities.

Much before any other kind of division, you can divide empaths into two broad categories:

1. Awakened Empaths
2. Unawakened Empaths

You might have heard about the things empaths can do, and they all look splendid. These stories have found elaborate space in popular pop-culture. Most of these programs portray empaths as telepaths, psychics, and fortune-tellers. These programs are putting false impressions on the mind of the unsuspecting audience. They make the fact believable that all empaths possess these powers and very well know how to use them.

Nothing can be farther from the truth.

Awakened Empaths

These are the individuals who have realized that they are different and that they possess a gift. Much before anything else, it is a must that an individual identifies the self. An awakened empath is an individual who acknowledges who he or she is. An awakened individual will not be perplexed at the rush of emotions felt all of a sudden without a provocation. An awakened empath would know the extent of powers possessed, as well as the limitations that come along with them.

These individuals are not unaware or unsure about themselves. They realize the things they can do and those they can't.

Being an empath is a gift, but it can only be so if one realizes it. Awakened empaths are those that know it and are always conscious about it.

They are the individuals who have a clear idea of their abilities, and they are continually working on honing them. Possessing an ability would mean nothing if the individual has no consciousness of it and never works on improving it. It is like a capable painter working as a car mechanic. Painting is a creative work, and repairing requires one to be methodical; it won't work well for that individual.

Clear identification of the ability and constant endeavor to enhance those abilities is the mark of an awakened empath.

The most important part of being an awakened empath is faith in the abilities possessed. The world can always doubt your skills as it doesn't see what an empath can see. However, an empath must never doubt those abilities, and then only they'll work. Unwavering faith in what you perceive to be your strength will make you an awakened empath.

Awakened empaths have the power to make a difference in the lives of people around them. They are the ones who know their abilities, trust them, and continually work to enhance them.

Such empaths have the charisma to stand out in the crowd. They are confident and can function smoothly in most conditions.

A skill most common in empaths is the ability to get an accurate first impression of a person they meet. Awakened empaths can usually assess the true nature of the people they meet more accurately than others. Their ability to sense the subtle energy and vibes behind the visual façade is responsible for that. They also possess powerful, intuitive skills.

In a nutshell, awakened empaths are confident and skilled individuals with the power to look deep inside the people they meet. They know their strengths and weaknesses, and hence they don't easily get overwhelmed by the emotions they feel.

Unawakened Empaths

As you could easily guess, unawakened empaths are the stark opposites of awakened empaths. They might possess similar abilities as awakened empaths. Still, because they neither realize their skills nor have control over them, they keep feeling crushed under the weight of those very abilities.

An awakened empath is like a person with a car driving uphill. Although he/she has to go up against gravity, the vehicle would help the empath go up. The system helps in the whole process. There is nothing to act against. Now imagine an awakened empath on that same road with a vehicle without the fuel. The task would become immensely tricky because the same car that was supposed to help would act as a piece of extra baggage.

The burden of carrying high sensitivities and powers is what makes the lives of unawaked empaths so challenging. They have a gift, but because they do not know of it, that gift becomes a burden.

Ordinary people fancy the powers they believe an empath has. Won't you feel lucky if you were in a position to know the real intent of a person in front of you in the first meeting itself? Won't that make business deals and negotiations so much easier?

That would be a bargain for most people in the world.

Imagine how wonderful it would be if you could sense the coming danger beforehand. We all want to have that reliable power of intuition that can warn us of all the bad things about to happen. Empaths have that power inbuilt. Yet, it'd make the life of an unawakened empath difficult as that individual would have no way to use that information or to trust it.

Being an empath is a gift. However, not realizing that you are an empath or not having control over your faculties can quickly turn into a curse.

CHAPTER 7
The Struggles Of Living As An Unawakened Empath

I have remained focused on the fact that unawaked empaths may have to lead a miserable life, and they'd find no way out of it. The reason for emphasizing this fact is significant. However small the exclusive group of empaths may look, when you look at the number in absolute terms, you won't be able to ignore it.

The empaths are not more than 1 to 2 percent of the total population. Although this looks like a very insignificant percentage, when you look at it in absolute terms, hundreds of millions of people across the globe fall under this category.

Such a large percentage of the population with a confused and vulnerable state of feelings and emotions isn't good news. The problem doesn't just end there. If the people with a sensitive, emotional state fell straight into one category, it would have been straightforward. However, that's not the case.

The percentage of highly sensitive people in the world is around 15 to 20 percent. It means a much bigger class of people are there with a somewhat resembling state of mind but without the abilities.

It becomes very easy for others as well as for the victims themselves to consider themselves as just being emotionally vulnerable. However, they go far beyond being emotionally vulnerable. They are not only prone to get emotionally hurt very quickly, but they also act as emotional sponges. It means they'd keep absorbing the pain and suffering of others and may not understand the way to deal with the surge of emotions.

They'd keep having intuitions, premonitions, weird dreams, and psychic sightings but wouldn't know what to make of it. In such a scenario, these very powers can turn into nightmares for the victims.

An unawakened empath may keep living a miserable life as that individual would be lifting the weight of emotional, psychological, and sometimes even physical pain of people around. That person would also remain crushed under the influence of abilities that are beyond his/her control.

From early childhood, empaths begin experiencing these powers. In the beginning, it isn't that difficult as people don't call you mad for behaving differently or talking things that may sound nonsense to them. But, as you advance in age, your experiences remain the same, but the rest of the world begins to think that you haven't grown.

It is a reason most unawakened empaths experience confusion, anxiety, and inability to regulate their emotions. They are never able to adjust to others. They feel exhausted in crowds but are never able to identify the real cause.

Empaths, awakened or unawakened, can feel negative energies. However, unawakened empaths are never able to ascertain what to make out of that feeling. As a result, they are unable to distance themselves from those negative energies and end up being miserable.

One of the biggest problems is their inability to manage their energy fields. Empaths are porous, and they act like sponges when it comes to absorbing feelings and emotions of others around them. Awakened empaths understand this crucial fact, and the most important thing they learn is to differentiate between an emotion that originated within them and the one that doesn't belong to them. In this way, they can prevent unwanted emotional overload and also help the people in need.

Whereas, an unawakened empath wouldn't be able to carry out this crucial differentiation and hence remain crushed under the burden of those emotions.

Unawakened empaths usually suffer from a lack of confidence. The power of intuition is the biggest asset of empaths. Awakened empaths know they can rely on their intuition as they have faith in their capabilities. Unawakened empaths lack this confidence, and hence they are always dangling between logic and intuition. Self-doubt and confusion become a permanent feature in their lives.

They are afraid of groups but long for friendships and love. This longing can also become a problem for them because their desire for love makes them rely on others too much. They become easy targets for exploitation, and narcissistic people take full advantage of this.

They remain trapped in their web of assumptions while the world is never in sync with them.

Being an Empath Isn't a Choice

Being an empath isn't a choice that you get. It may run in your genes and hence keeps getting passed on as a legacy—some people empaths in many different circumstances, like after having near-death experiences or severe accidents. But, it is never by choice that you get to become an empath.

However, it is always in your control to determine what you make of your abilities.

You can keep living the life of an unawakened empath and remain a subject of personal ridicule. Unawakened empaths have weak personal boundaries, and hence they always remain vulnerable to absorbing feelings and emotions of others.

The most dangerous aspect of these problems is to give in to addictions and other methods to become numb to such influx.

It is common for empaths to feel overwhelmed with emotions, feel hurt, uncomfortable, emotionally unsafe, shy, anxious, exhausted, and drained. Self-pity, over criticism and self-criticism, too many rejections, fears, and other similar feelings may lead to insomnia and guilt. All these feelings can easily lead to the development of escapist tendencies.

The easy way to escape is to numb your senses or lower your sense of perception, and overdependence on alcohol, drugs, and gambling always looks attractive and comfortable options. Some people who do not go to such lengths try to find refuge in other things like food, shopping, or other such habits.

Empaths must understand that taking refuge in these addictions is an easy way out but a temporary recourse. It may cut you off from your problems momentarily, but they'd always be there.

The path to becoming an awakened empath may look tough in the beginning to some empaths, but it is the best way in the current scenario. For an unawakened empath to lead a satisfying life full of joy and normalcy, there is not a lot you'll need to do. Even if you begin acknowledging and accepting yourself as an empath, you'll find it much easier to live with your gift.

The sooner you develop the realization, the faster the doors to timely identification of feelings and emotions would begin. These are the most significant troubles in the lives of empaths. They keep getting bombarded by unsolicited emotions. They are unable to identify them and hence remain troubled.

Part of the process of turning into an awakened empath is to learn to differentiate. It will help if you learn to distinguish between your emotions and the emotions of others. Once the identification is clear, emotions coming from outside will not have a toll on your mental balance.

Another step is to get the fear of being an empath out of your mind. Empaths keep struggling with the emotional turmoil for a significant part of their lives. When they begin getting any help, they want to get rid of it. But, being an empath isn't a choice. You can't shake it off. It would be best if you learned to live with it.

Finding True Love Can Become Tricky

It is natural for all of us to desire love. The need for love and attention is even more significant in empaths. These individuals absorb more pain and suffering from their surroundings. Loved ones around them can help them in healing and provide positive energy. However, empaths may find it very difficult to get true love.

Being an empath is very tough, and living with one isn't something different than a roller-coaster ride. Empaths can easily get overwhelmed by the emotions and energies of the people around them. It can make them fearful of intimacy. They'd long for more and more along time, and this can bring a rift between relationships if the other partner fails to understand it. An awakened empath will know this need and discuss it with the partner to create a balance. However, unawakened empaths are unaware of this and hence end up in strained relationships.

All empaths have a natural ability to feel and absorb the emotions and feelings of others, and their partners are no exception. Here, it is essential to note that they are not discussing the emotions and feelings but absorbing them directly. Personal boundaries get trampled very easily. Unawakened empaths are never able to enforce these boundaries and find themselves in a fix.

Empaths feel more overwhelmed by emotions and need more alone time than others. Struggles with anxieties and depression are everyday affairs. They may get upset over tiny things and not know the reason for that, and such things can be tricky to understand for their partners.

All these things make the love lives of empaths increasingly tough. However, that doesn't end the need to have someone to love, and this is the weakness most often exploited by narcissists.

Narcissistic people often identify an empath's dependency and people-pleasing behavior and use it to their advantage. They keep playing with the vulnerabilities of empaths.

Unawakened empaths especially need to remain aware of toxic relationships as they are prone to fall into their trap. These relationships can become a significant emotional drain on them, and they may find themselves in deep trouble.

CHAPTER 8
Unraveling The Nature Of An Empath

As I have also mentioned earlier, it can be challenging to put empaths in a single rigid frame. All empaths may not show the same signs or all the signs and traits, and hence defining the true nature of an empath in a single frame isn't possible.

There are several signs and traits that empaths exhibit, and only an empath can understand whether he/she possesses them or not.

If you search on the internet, you can easily find hundreds of signs and traits of empaths. However, even ordinary people can find a number of those traits within themselves on some self-introspection.

Not only this, but several personality tests on the internet can also term you as an empath.

Do those sound believable? Yes.

Are they correct? In 99% cases, No.

You must understand that empaths aren't mutants, and hence if you broaden the traits or soften them up a tad bit more, a considerable number of people would get included in that category.

Most people who aren't empaths and do not have those struggles that empaths face are mesmerized by the powers possessed by empaths as portrayed in TV programs. This fascination makes them want to believe that they also possess those traits but never have realized them. The innate desire to have those powers and feel special makes them think so.

Now, there are several characteristics like a desire to spend time in nature, easy to manipulate, free-spirited, hates injustice, and other such things can't be defining traits.

Most of us living in concrete jungles like to spend time in nature. Even for the most conservative of the individuals, it'd be hard to digest the fact that they aren't free-spirited, and none of us would like to believe that we love injustice. At least on a personal scale, we all love justice.

These can not be the defining traits of an empath because they are very general.

There will be some traits that are not very general, and yet even they may not be very accurate because even **Hyper Sensitive People (HSP)** would also have those traits.

For instance, a defining trait of empaths is that they are highly sensitive individuals, but so are HSPs. As far as being sensitive is concerned, empaths and HSPs can be equally responsive to feelings and emotions. The real difference lies in the qualities beyond that. HSPs are sensitive to sensory-stimulating signals like light, sound, and temperature. They may feel exhausted at crowded places and like to live alone.

HSPs are sensitive to feelings and emotions but may be unable to process them further. An empath may go much beyond merely feeling those emotions; it absorbs them. The company of a grieving individual will not only make an empath sad like an HSV, but the empath may also experience that same loss within.

Feeling the pain and emotions of people around them is a gift empaths share with HSPs. However, they have the additional ability to feel energy. They can absorb and internalize subtle energies emanating from the people or environment around them.

Defining Characteristic Traits of Empaths

Highly Sensitive

It is the bone of contention. It has been an issue that has created the highest amount of confusion. There is no measure of sensitivity, and it is subjective, like pain and pleasure.

Simply being sensitive wouldn't make a person an empath. Anyone can be shy, introverted, and vulnerable to feelings and emotions.

Empaths take sensitivity to another level. Being sensitive not only means getting affected by the environment around, but it also means to read even the slightest difference in it. An empath would also be able to sense the façade of faces people wear quickly. They have the innate ability to feel the pain and emotions of the people around them. It means, when an empath is around you, words may not be needed to express your sorrow or discomfort to the empath. An empath would be able to feel it within himself/herself.

The sensitivities are physical, emotional, as well as spiritual. An empath may also be able to feel the presence of various kinds of energies around them.

Very Sharp Instincts

Empaths have very sharp instincts. It is something that empaths possess with distinction. Empaths have a very keen sense of intuition, and it is something that can be a boon as well as a curse.

The power of intuition is a widely debated subject.

It might have happened with you several times that you knew what was coming. There are times when, before making a decision, your instinct is telling you to do something else. You go with your logic, and in the end, the result is terrible.

We all have this gut feeling, and we all are troubled by it because it is mostly directing you against logic. It leads to self-doubt, confusion, and anxiety.

Now think of a person who is getting these intuitive thoughts more strongly and all the time. Awakened empaths know that they can trust these thoughts, and their life becomes somewhat easy. However, most unawakened empaths are never able to trust their intuition, and hence they keep feeling the confusion and anxiety.

The power of intuition is an asset that an empath has. Most people have this power of intuition, but it is neither too specific nor reliable enough. An awakened empath would have high confidence over this power of intuition and would be able to do much with it.

Unawakened empaths would also have this power of intuition, but they'll neither be able to trust these signals nor act against them. It will create a lot of confusion and doubt.

It is a distinguishing trait of an empath. Empaths don't just have ordinary intuitions like the rest of the people around them, but their intuitions are deep and defined.

Ability to Absorb Emotions and Feelings

It is another distinguishing characteristic trait that most empaths possess. An empath can easily absorb the feelings and emotions of other people around them. They don't need to talk or with those individuals. It can happen even by looking at pictures or videos.

Now, this can be a very damaging quality to have. Imagine you are having a great time at a diner with someone special. Someone you have been longing to meet. Everything has been going great, and all of a sudden, someone with deep wounds passes by. You'd feel that pain and sorrow within you. The joy and exuberance would evaporate, and sadness would engulf you.

It isn't a hypothetical situation but a reality of the life of most empaths. Enjoying life in public can be very difficult for them because there can be no control over the feelings, emotions, and energies that you may encounter.

Can you recall any such incident happening with you?

Empaths will have a long list of such incidents where they felt deep sorrow within themselves without any provocation. Everything would have been going perfect, and they'll suddenly feel overwhelmed by the surge of contrasting emotions.

It is a reality most empaths have to learn to deal with in their personal lives.

The surge of emotions that they absorb is generally so strong that it becomes challenging to distinguish whether the feelings are their own or of someone else.

The problem is so significant because it is happening all the time. We can't live in a box. We are social beings, and meeting and interacting with others is a need. It is also the most significant cause of discomfort.

Aversion from Crowded Places

It is a point that would need several qualifiers. Introverts hate crowded places as they don't like to interact with others. HSPs don't want to go to crowded places as such places make them feel drained. Many people, in general, have a dislike for overcrowded places. Does that qualify all those as empaths?

You can't use the disliking of crowded places as a characteristic feature. Empaths don't like overcrowded places because they feel overwhelmed by the surge of emotions they begin absorbing.

Empaths are generally introverts, but many empaths aren't. Being an introvert isn't the real cause for their aversion to crowded places. The emotional overload that they experience at those places is the real culprit. At crowded places, the empaths get bombarded by a variety of feelings and emotions possessed by people around them. They begin acting as magnets. It isn't the fault of the crowd but their inability to keep such emotions away.

Even the extrovert empaths who enjoy the company of others can begin feeling exhausted in the crowds because it isn't their external demeanor that's getting challenged but the internal emotion processing mechanism.

Fear Intimate Relationships But Long for Love

It may sound paradoxical for many people, but this is a reality of life for empaths. Empaths deeply desire love. Empaths continually get bombarded by emotions from all sides, and this does cause a lot of damage. They become emotionally vulnerable. Love is a magical potion that can help them heal. If there is someone whom they can trust and rely upon, it becomes easier for them to recover.

However, most of the time, they are not able to sustain their relationships.

Empaths want love, companionship, togetherness, but they also need their me-time to recuperate. When they find someone who loves them, they usually begin getting smothered by love and don't get the breathing space they need.

Most people are unable to understand their exact need for love as well as some alone time.

If the person they love is too possessive, overpowering, or demanding, empaths will begin feeling suffocated.

It is the reason failed relationships can quickly become a regular feature in the lives of empaths. Ordinary people usually never get to see this aspect of their lives when they aspire to become empaths or have their powers.

Empaths Long for the Me-Time

As we have already discussed in the previous point, the me-time is a must for empaths. It is the time needed to recover from all the pain and suffering they might have experienced.

Awakened or unawakened, being an empath is never going to be easy. An empath is bound to experience emotional pain and suffering that others might never know. Their experience of such emotions is going to be very wide. Personal pain doesn't mire their lives. They are always suffering from the pain of others.

Getting over such pain would always need a lot of effort. It is the reason they need alone time. It can't be done in the company of others because then the constant absorption of energy would keep taking place.

The alone time is very soothing for empaths. It isn't the time they are getting bored or missing something but getting healed from within.

It is a thing that distinguishes the need for alone time in empaths from others. They are not trying to run away from the world like introverts when they seek seclusion, but they are just healing internally.

Empaths are Soft Targets for Energy Vampires

It is a hard reality of the lives of empaths that they always need to be cautious of energy vampires. They can never be too careless in scrutinizing people around them.

If you carefully look around yourself, you'll find several toxic people around you that may be a drain on your energy. These are energy vampires.

Energy vampires are the people around who feel entitled. They don't take accountability for anything and may hold others responsible for everything that's going wrong.

Empaths are easy targets for energy vampires.

In the regular course of life, everyone gets attacked by toxic people who act as energy vampires. However, most people can easily avoid such influences. Various kinds of vampires, like narcissists and rageaholics, can have a profound impact on the mental and emotional balance of empaths.

People with narcissistic attitudes are challenging to deal with most people, but they can be big trouble for empaths as they are emotionally vulnerable.

Such energy vampires are easily able to overpower the empaths emotionally. They can make the empaths feel worthless and incapable of being loved. Self-pity and gloom can begin taking over the heart of an empath, causing further damage and pushing the empaths towards addictions.

Greenery and Nature is Replenishing for Empaths

It is also a frequently misinterpreted characteristic. Most people living in the concrete jungles love greenery and the lap of nature, as it is a refreshing change. However, it isn't the same for empaths. They need natural surroundings to heal themselves.

Human beings are different. We all have different emotional makeup and personal boundaries. Most of the time, the exchange of feelings and emotions is also one-sided. It means, while an empath may be able to absorb the emotions and feelings of others, there is no way to transfer them elsewhere, and hence the empath has to live with that burden.

While it is easy to absorb emotion due to the porous nature of the self, it isn't possible to transfer them to other individuals with the same ease.

However, that's not the case with plants and nature. Nature is simple. It is absorbing and forgiving. Empaths find it very easy to pass on their burden of emotions and feelings to the plants and other natural objects silently, and it is very healing.

It is a reason empaths love nature so much and need to go in natural surroundings very often to replenish themselves.

One shouldn't get confused between nature lovers and empaths.

Weak Personal Boundaries

One of the most significant weaknesses of empaths is their inability to have boundaries. No matter what kind of an empath a person is, having firm personal boundaries is not a trait to be found.

Most people would feel the sting of watching a car crash victim. But, an empath may feel crushed. Most people wouldn't mind walking past a homeless person begging on the streets. If an ordinary person's heart weeps, he/she will give some money to the beggar and walk past. If possible, an empath would certainly give money, but even after that, wouldn't be able to forget the pain the beggar has been feeling long after leaving the scene.

Weak personal boundaries are a substantial reason empaths have poor relationships. Empaths can look into the heart and mind of the person they love, and they keep doing that without respecting the boundaries. It eliminates dialogue from the relationships and brings encroachment. It can crush relationships.

Empaths find it very hard to say 'no' to anyone. This tendency can lead to overexploitation, which most empaths suffer.

Empaths have Very Strong Senses

It is a natural trait that most empaths share with HSPs. Both have powerful senses of smell and taste. HSPs are introverts, but empaths can also be very talkative. Their ability to listen is also very sharp, and some may also be able to see much better than others. The ability to view better has less to do with the quality of vision but more with objectivity. They have a sharp eye, and they miss very little even when they are just looking at things with a cursory eye.

These are some of the traits that are common in empaths. However, this list is by no means exhaustive as empaths are of various kinds. A telepathic empath will have profound communication abilities. Dream empaths will be able to remember their dreams well and then deduce meaning from them.

Like everything else, being an empath also comes with its positives and negatives. It is up to the empath to make good of them or keep rotting in them.

Being an empath isn't something straightforward. You get a gift and also a responsibility to hone that gift, or that same gift can become a headache for you.

Empaths are Very Generous and Mostly Unable to Say 'No'

Being generous is a quality most people like to have in them of the people around them. But, empaths take generosity to the next level.
They have a people-pleasing attitude, and they try to go to any extent to make people around them happy. It is a trait that makes them susceptible to exploitation. Some people understand their desire to be the savior and begin exploiting them.
Empaths generally find it very hard to say no to anyone. Many people take advantage of this weakness, and empaths still keep serving.

CHAPTER 9
What Does It Mean To Be An Empath?

Being an empath isn't something you can shake off. If you are an empath, then every area in your life will get affected by it. You can't expect to have the good things of being an empath and leave out the bad ones. If being an empath gives you the ability to know about the feelings and emotions of loved ones, you will also need to remain prepared to get bombarded by feelings and emotions of the people you encounter on the roads and your workplace. It won't be a choice.

Being an empath has a profound impact on every area of life. From your health to your love-life and work, being an empath affects everything. You can't expect to have an ordinary life like regular people. You will have your unique challenges and opportunities that you'll need to learn to handle.

Health

Health of an empath gets the hardest impact. You can be an empath of any type. Your abilities as an empath may empower your dreams, your intuition, your telepathic skills, or something else. As you can see, most of these abilities have to do with your mind. However, that doesn't mean that they won't affect your physical, emotional, or mental health.

Being an empath makes you a receptive person. Awakened empaths have more definite personal boundaries, and therefore, they get less affected by energies around them, and unawakened empaths have weaker limits, and they get affected more. But, they all get influenced, nonetheless. The only difference being, awakened empaths have more definite personal boundaries, and hence they can manage the influences better and are better in overcoming the challenges.

Even awakened empaths can't prevent the absorption of feelings, emotions, and energies. Just that, they are better at distinguishing the emotions and feelings that belong to them and the ones that don't. At the same time, unawakened empaths find it increasingly difficult to manage the constant bombardment of emotions and feelings as they can't differentiate between theirs and others.

It also has a profound impact on an empath's work life and outside interactions. Irrespective of your state of consciousness, venturing out would remain tricky. You are bound to get bombarded by a string of emotions and feelings when in crowded places. It will make you feel exhausted and drained. It is a sort of occupational hazard as it comes with being an empath. It would help if you learned to deal with it properly.

Environments with very high sensory stimulation also don't work well for empaths. For instance, an empath may not find dance clubs with loud music very attractive. There will be too much noise and physical touch involved. It can leave them overstimulated. As an empath, you must keep in mind to avoid such places as much as possible.

Physical contact of any form must be strictly avoided as far as possible by all kinds of empaths. It doesn't mean that you can't shake hands with others or hug your loved ones. It merely means that shaking hands with people you don't know shouldn't become a thing for you. It may be a norm for others and socially accepted greeting, but it can be an energy drain for an empath. While you may feel energized by shaking hands or hugging someone you love and appreciate, shaking hands or hugging someone you don't know might suck up your energy. Finding alternate ways to greet people would be better for empaths. They can greet people with folded hands as done in eastern cultures or bow down a little.

If you are an emotional empath, then it will be natural to get affected even profoundly as your body would be more receptive to emotions, feelings, and energies. You'd need more practice in distinguishing between various emotions getting absorbed. As an emotional empath, it'd be impossible for you to prevent the absorption of energies; however, if you can increase your interaction with people having positive vibes, you can benefit from them. As an empath, you are going to absorb energy nonetheless. Let it be a positive energy in the equal proportions that you get, and it will make healing much more manageable.

Being a physical empath isn't going to be any easier. A physical empath can pick the physical pain and suffering of the people around them. It means if you are around someone having skin rashes, you can expect to get some yourself. It calls for extra caution. However, there is also an upside to it. If you come in contact with healthy individuals full of positive energies, you may even get a part of that and thrive on it. It is a miraculous power.

Although it is easier to prescribe mixing with a select group of people, we all know that it isn't possible for all extent and purposes. We will meet all sorts of people and will be able to exercise limited control. Hence, it would help if you remained more vigilant about your mental state.

Low energy levels, anxieties, sadness, and mild stress are some of the milder symptoms to depict a toll on your health. If you are continually living in a negative or not in a conducive environment, you might get these symptoms without any remarkable or apparent cause. It should work as a signal that you need to make some immediate changes in your company, or you need to beef us your boundaries.

If you do not pay attention to these, they can result in severe anxieties, depression, and rage.

Staying for too long in a charged atmosphere is never advised for an empath as it can be very imposing on the personality of the empath.

Staying at the top of the physical, mental, and emotional state is a must for an empath because they are bound to carry some extra burden at the end of the day. If they begin the day under a lot of stress, it can seriously impede their performance.

Because being an empath isn't a disease, there is no medicine for it. However, there are ways to enhance personal boundaries and prevent invading emotions from affecting your mental and emotional health.

A healthy diet with a lot of green vegetables and fruits will provide you the energy and stamina to ward of the usual stress. You must also practice meditation daily as that can help you in stabilizing your mind and your heart even in the most aggravating circumstances.

If you are feeling overwhelmed by emotions and do not feel like taking extra burden, you must recuse yourself and stay in solitude or the lap of nature until you heal completely.

Empaths must deal with their health issues, in general, very promptly. Ignoring these issues can have a long-term impact on physical, mental, and emotional health, and recovery may be tenuous and tedious, if at all possible.

Love, Relationships, and Sexual Life

These are essential concerns of life, and an empath may struggle in all of them if they do not deal with them appropriately. We all long for true love and stable relationships in life. They help us become better people. However, we all know the outcome of fake love and toxic relationships. Even an emotionally stable person would find it very hard to get out of a toxic relationship. The more harmful they are, the harder it becomes to get away from them. It can be an ordeal for an empath who will undoubtedly have greater appeal for people who are dependent on them or need them. They have the innate desire to act as a savior, and that thinking can be disastrous for them.

Due to the importance of all three aspects, we'll discuss them one by one.

>**Love:** Love is the magical potion that can heal the aching heart of an empath. An empath is always longing for love as it is getting filled with pain, sorrow, hatred, and other such dark emotions of people around. The company of a loved one can help an empath energize and heal. An empath will feel much better in the company of someone he/she enjoys being with and trusts completely.
>
>However, while an empath's heart is always aching for the company of someone he/she loves, too much intimacy can become overkill. Empaths want to be loved, but they also want their alone time. Usually, the people who love you are too much concerned about you, and they invade your space unknowingly; this can cause real trouble.
>
>Although it may not be a problem for an awakened empath who understands this need and discusses it openly with the loved

ones, the unawakened empaths usually get caught in the fix. They aren't even aware of the need, and that can lead to misunderstandings, mistrusts, and loss of love.

It is a must that an empath understands the unique circumstances he/she is in and discusses it with the loved ones before any rift arises. Being open, direct, yet considerate is the only solution to find a middle ground. Although this is an ideal solution, most empaths would find it very difficult to arrive at it.

Empaths may also feel emotionally spent most of the time, and hence they might not be able to contribute a lot. It can make the other person feel odd. However, empaths would have to communicate this to their loved ones and explain the way things are in their lives. Chances are once they understand, love would flourish easily. The complication lies in the level of communication and understanding. Most empaths can understand the needs and feelings of others without the use of words. They can remain in the delusion that even others can do the same and hence not use words to communicate their situation correctly. It is the reason for most miscommunication.

Relationships: Nobody throws an open invitation to narcissists like empaths. It is in their nature to feel drawn towards people in need of love and support. Narcissists are damaged people who like to suck up all the positive energy in the person trying to support them, and the empaths may even feel that. Still, they'd find it increasingly difficult to distance themselves from selfish or narcissistic people. Narcissists give them a sense of purpose as they know they are needed a lot there.

It is the reason, empaths who have such a robust, intuitive self feel impulsively drawn towards narcissists and toxic relationships. Such relationships rapidly become abusive, and empaths know that they are getting exploited. However, they are not able to resist the temptation of another try.

Empaths have an innate desire to help the people in need, and they need to understand that there is a limit to what they can do. They cannot keep on suffering at the hands of their tormentors and keep going back.

Relationships can act as an elixir in the lives of empaths. A healthy relationship with a good-hearted individual can help empaths function with great ease and confidence. On the other hand, a narcissist can continually make them feel inferior and inadequate. They'd keep getting hurt inside out and wouldn't get time to heal their hearts.

Empaths would need to understand the importance of relationships in their lives and the roles they can play. They'd need to be extra careful while building relationships and not compromise on the critical aspects of finding correct people for relationships.

Sex: It is an aspect that's generally not discussed much. However, ignoring sex can be a big mistake. Empaths treat sex in a very different way than ordinary people. For empaths, sex is a medium to release the pressure built inside them and not just a way to express their love to the partner.

It is where the rift begins.

While most people want sex to be a beautiful expression of love, the way empaths treat sex and indulge in the act; it looks as if they are using the sexual act for physical gratification. It is leaning more on the side of lust and less on the emotional side of it.

Most of the time, their sexual partners are not able to understand this distinction, and they begin to feel like an object of sexual gratification. The usual instinct is to deprive empaths of sex, and that can lead to frustration, emotional outbursts, and further rifts.

The things are not as they may seem to the partners of empaths. An empath will usually not engage in a sexual relationship with an individual whom he/she doesn't love. One must understand that love is the basis of that sexual act. However, empaths may not be able to portray that accurately while they engage in sexual activity.

It is the responsibility of the empaths to explain their need for sexual release and its importance for them. Even after that, their partners may not be able to provide them comparable sexual gratification, but as long as there is proper communication, things can work smoothly.

Work

Work is the third most crucial front an empath needs to deal with in life. Crowded places or places filled with charged people can be challenging for empaths. However, this may not be a choice for empaths working in highly competitive environments. When an empath has to work at places where there is a lot of excitement, rush, stress, or other such excitable feelings floating in the air, they end up soaking the emotions of a lot of people and hoard them in the form of stress, anxiety, and panic.

Such a thing can affect their performance to a great extent as well as their behavior at the workplace.

Avoiding charged atmospheres or crowded workplaces may not be possible for empaths, but they can still learn to maintain some distance. Empaths need to understand that they can't keep absorbing emotions and energies and still perform at their best. They will have to make suitable adjustments.

It is always best to avoid heated debates in offices and try to find as much alone time as possible. The longer you can work on your desk all alone, the easier it would be for you to get over the absorbed energies.

You can also keep some plants and natural things on your workstation that can help in passing on the emotions and energies.

Regular meditation can play a fantastic role in keeping you centered and grounded even after staying in charged atmospheres for long. If you practice meditation regularly, you'll be able to enforce firm boundaries around you and also distinguish between the emotions and feelings that are yours and the ones you've absorbed from your surroundings.

Addictions

Until now, we have been discussing important things for a fruitful life of empaths. We have discussed the main areas of life that concern them the most.

Unfortunately, all empaths are not so fortunate to overcome all the issues. Their energy management is weak, and they do not get the release they need. Such empaths may also repeatedly fail in relationships and get exploited by narcissists and dominator energy vampires.

Such empaths find an easy way out in addictions. Alcohol, drugs, gambling, and sex is the usual way to numb the sensations and find some peace.

It is a path on which empaths find the ease and release they have been looking for all their lives.

They want the constant bombardment of emotions to stop, and that can't happen until they are in an inebriated state. It begins as an excuse and quickly becomes an addiction that they would find extremely difficult to leave.

The chemicals consumed may help in the intoxication of the mind and numbing of the senses but don't solve the problems causing them. The relief is momentary and false. Giving in to addictions is like trying to find brightness at the end of a dead tunnel.

Alcohol, drugs, and gambling are just some mediums that usually get most of the bad press. However, they are not the only addictions.

Many empaths begin finding solace in food and get addicted to food. They aren't eating food to fill their tummies but to absorb their pain and divert their attention from their current problems. Comfort foods, high sugar foods like desserts, especially become their favorite as high sugar content leads to serotonin release in the brain that makes us feel good.

Some empaths try to find solace and joy in shopping. As long as they remain immersed in shopping, they can divert their attention from the current issues. However, we all know that this trick doesn't work well in the long-term.

The sense of solace, joy, and fulfillment can never come for an empath from such addictions. These can only act as temporary diversions.

Instead, these addictions can open the floodgates of sorrowful existence, severe anxiety, and depression.

Trying to find a way through these addictions can be as harmful as self-medicating yourself while suffering from a terminal illness. The medication will not only lead to further pain and suffering, but you'll also live always in fear of something terrible happening in the end.

The best way out is to seek help. The best way out for an empath is to talk to someone you trust or take professional advice. There should be no shame in seeking help because, as an empath, you have immense potential, but that can be getting washed down the drain due to poor management.

Addictive behavior is destructive in its own right and harmful for everyone, in general. Getting out of addictions can be particularly tricky for empaths due to their impulsive nature.

However, if they engage in more productive ways to channelize their energies through mediums like exercise and meditation, they can get much better results. Meditation is a fantastic way to center your mind and lives. It helps in grounding, and you'll be able to manage your faculties better.

Getting out of unhealthy addictions should be a priority for any empath because it is only going to drag you deeper into the much from where extraction may become nearly impossible.

Psychic Abilities

In the end, we come to the topic that may have the interest of all the people who want to have powers like empaths. The empaths have to live a life ridden with deep fissures, and no one can accurately understand their pain in the real sense.

For all the trouble they have to go through and all the positivity, love, and compassion for which they are a medium, nature endows them with several powers that ordinary people can only desire.

One of the most common abilities in empaths is their power of intuition. Everyone has some intuitive capability, but in ordinary people, this power of intuition is very subdued.

They may be able to feel things about to come but have no reason to rely on that information, and there is never really any confirmation. Most of the time, what they think as their intuition is just a flight or fight response originating in a gut inspiring them to take the escape route. However, that's not the case with empaths.

The intuitive ability in empaths is generally highly pronounced. Although this power of intuition may keep the unawakened empaths confused, the awakened empaths know for sure that they can completely trust their intuition.

Now it may only seem like an added asset to an outsider, but most people would be willing to swap a lot to have such power of intuition. Imagine the kind of dangers you can dodge if you could even have a real clue about them. Empaths get this power by default.

This ability is just not limited to having some wild hunches, but many empaths also can see events far off in the future. They may have it as premonitions. It is a miracle, but if you have faith in your powers and the heart set in the right place, your consciousness can get connected to the collective consciousness of all the other beings and make such visions possible.

Some empaths can heal others not only emotionally and mentally but also physically. It is a power that can make you the most wanted person in your circle. Although it comes at the high cost of your health and well being, yet it is a power that can help people in certain specialized professions in assessing and understanding the ailments suffered by others more accurately. The ability to absorb wounds and illnesses and provide healing is a truth and not a mere hoax.

Some empaths can have vivid dreams that can unlock the secrets of past and future events. Some empath dreamers can accurately decipher the sleep-visions of others and explain their meanings.

Some empaths can sense energies around them and successfully interact with them. It might sound absurd to many, but for them, even the whole idea of empaths may look silly. Nevertheless, it is a possibility for some empaths. Not only this, but some empaths can also communicate with energies on the other side and ghosts.

Some empaths can easily read the minds of people in front. Some empaths don't even need words or a medium to communicate as they can connect telepathically.

These are all possibilities that become a reality for an empath, but they have a cost. An empath can neither ask for them, and most empaths don't even desire them.

These abilities are within empaths, but they do need to work on them and sharpen the skills.

An empath must understand that being an empath is neither a gift nor a curse. It is a condition with which most empaths are born with and have to learn to handle.

Once you have the gift, there is no turning back. Either you can learn to utilize it to its full potential and make the lives of others better and benefit from the satisfaction it gives, or you can keep sulking over your woes of being an empath.

Irrespective of the ability an empath gets, it is the responsibility of an empath to help others. That's something for which the heart of an empath always bleeds. Most unawakened empaths remain ignorant of such urges within them and keep ignoring them. However, whether you recognize the gift you have or not, it is going to be there.

If you are prudent enough to realize that gift, you'll be making your own as well as the lives of others easy. Some empaths do not recognize their powers and responsibilities and fall prey to their vulnerabilities or take the destructive path.

CHAPTER 10
Do You Think You Are An Empath?

It is a fact that the correct identification of an empath is difficult. There are scores of personality tests available on the internet that may identify most people as empaths. They fail to differentiate between people having empathy and real empaths.

Even ordinary people have empathy. It is in human nature to have empathy and compassion towards others. That doesn't make a person an empath.

It creates another problem that most people undermine. Due to this incorrect identification and no proper way to identify a real empath, most empaths are unable to realize their unique nature, abilities, responsibilities, and the requirements to recognize their gift.

The utter confusion, self-pity, and helplessness that ensues make the life of empaths pitiful.

As we have already discussed this plenty of times in this book, being an empath isn't a problem, a curse, or a disease. However, not realizing that you are an empath can lead to miseries.

An unawakened empath will have to live trapped under the burden of being an empath. That individual will have no other option than to bear the indiscriminate and unsolicited bombardment of emotions and feelings and won't even have firm boundaries. Realization is the first step towards course correction, and hence it is imperative that you accurately identify whether you possess the traits of an empath or not.

While trying to assess whether they are an empath or not, most people make a crucial mistake. They try to look in the wrong direction. They are mostly looking for the abilities empaths possess. If that is the path you were going to take, you are bound to be disappointed.

It'd be better if you understand that an unawakened empath will most likely possess all the problems an empath faces and least likely to have any of the abilities.

The reason is simple. You don't need practice to exhibit weaknesses while you need to practice a lot to master a skill. Training can't help you in acquiring any power that empaths possess, but it'll help you in enhancing those abilities.

It is also essential to understand that even at the height of being a fully awakened empath, you are not going to have the famed powers of spiderman, superman, or any other cartoon character that wears underwear over pants.

Jokes apart, empathic abilities help you in enhancing your sensory or cognitive powers to a level not possible for ordinary beings.

The simple purpose of this chapter is to make you understand whether you have the underlying symptoms of an empath. If you feel that you own several systems of an empath, it will help you know the cause of the problems experienced, here onwards, you can begin working on them.

There are some straightforward questions that you need to ask yourself and come up with an honest answer. Try to be as critical as possible in those answers. You must understand that the correct reply to those questions can help you in getting out of the mental and emotional trap that you might feel caught up in at the moment.

It would help if you answered these questions without an expectation of a gain or the fear of a loss.

Do you think you are incredibly moody and suffer from depression or anxiety?

An empath can have a cacophony of emotions inside, while everything on the outside may seem to be perfect. Everyone else can use noise cancellation headphones to cancel out the loud noises and focus on the objective. Empaths can find no way to do so with the constant bombardment of emotions happening inside. All this can make their moods volatile.

Most empaths don't even get to know the source of emotions and feelings they are having at that moment. Now, think of yourself in that position. Being in a perfectly pleasant setting and enjoying time with your loved ones and all of a sudden, gloom overshadow your mind. It strikes you like lightning, and you can't even tell why it has engulfed you. Has that ever happened with you?

Such emotional explosions are everyday occurrences for empaths because they can absorb emotions from people around them. Not only this, but they can also feel the emotions with the same intensity as the characters in the movie or program might have felt if it was a reality.

Have you ever felt like an emotional sponge?

When an individual has to go through such a string of emotions on a day to day basis, the development of anxiety and depression is usual.

Have you ever felt anxious about the sudden changes in mood or emotions while in the company of some loved one?

In such situations, you begin to feel as if you are losing complete control over the situation. There is a looming fear that things might go out of your hand anytime. Unless they already haven't gone out of control.

All this can lead to severe anxieties and depression in unawakened empaths. It can be too much to handle for the people who don't know the real cause of such emotional turbulence.

If you feel that you fit in this description, you have one qualification of an empath.

An empath can have a cacophony of emotions inside, while everything on the outside may seem to be perfect. Everyone else can use noise cancellation headphones to cancel out the loud noises and focus on the objective. Empaths can find no way to do so with the constant bombardment of emotions happening inside. All this can make their moods volatile.

Most empaths don't even get to know the source of emotions and feelings they are having at that moment. Now, think of yourself in that position. Being in a perfectly pleasant setting and enjoying time with your loved ones and all of a sudden, gloom overshadow your mind. It strikes you like lightning, and you can't even tell why it has engulfed you. Has that ever happened with you?

Such emotional explosions are everyday occurrences for empaths because they can absorb emotions from people around them. Not only this, but they can also feel the emotions with the same intensity as the characters in the movie or program might have felt if it was a reality.

Have you ever felt like an emotional sponge?

When an individual has to go through such a string of emotions on a day to day basis, the development of anxiety and depression is usual.

Have you ever felt anxious about the sudden changes in mood or emotions while in the company of some loved one?

In such situations, you begin to feel as if you are losing complete control over the situation. There is a looming fear that things might go out of your hand anytime. Unless they already haven't gone out of control.

All this can lead to severe anxieties and depression in unawakened empaths. It can be too much to handle for the people who don't know the real cause of such emotional turbulence.

If you feel that you fit in this description, you have one qualification of an empath.

Are your mood swings erratic and without the backing of a probable cause?

It is again just a question to confirm the previous point. Do you often have mood swings out of the blue?

Most people might find this question odd because the mood swings are, by default, out of the blue. However, even in that case, people do have a basis for mood swings. When they are upset, deep down, they know the thought that's troubling them. They have the backing of experience to support that emotion, and that experience is causing the pain.

In the case of empaths, there is no backing of the experience. The experience causing the mood swings would be missing in its entirety. There would be no probable cause for your sorrow. You are merely feeling sorrowful for the pain in the world.

If that is the case with you, you must pay attention to other symptoms as well.

Do you often feel like a misfit?

It is not an accurate description of an empath. I want to say categorically that empaths are not misfits.

However, you cannot deny the fact that until empaths discover their true identity and powers, most of them feel like misfits. They can't sit in groups, and they don't feel comfortable in crowds. They get emotionally overwhelmed on petty things and, most of the time, even without a cause. These many things are enough to brand them as misfits, but the list doesn't end here.

Empaths have a completely different outlook of things, and working for the self is not one of them. Their heart is always bleeding for others while they are themselves in a petty state. Even then, they are more concerned about others. It also makes them a fit case to be branded as misfits.

Do you feel like you are a misfit?

Have you ever thought that you look at things from a completely different perspective than others?

If that is the case, exploring deep may be useful for you.

Do you have a very low tolerance for heated arguments and yelling?

Empaths are highly sensitive beings. We have already discussed this in several forms, and yet we will again keep coming back to this topic as it has the essence.

Empaths, in general, have a very low tolerance to heated arguments, loud noises, and yelling. You will rarely find even an extrovert empath in such settings.

Empaths may have a view about things, but they'd generally keep it to themselves and certainly avoid getting into heated arguments. They have a very low tolerance to loud noises and yelling because when someone is screaming, the atmosphere gets charged with emotions, and it subsequently begins inflaming the feelings and emotions of the empath.

Either it is an awakened empath or an unawakened empath, you'll find both trying to avoid heated arguments, debates, and people who engage in too much yelling and screaming. It is always an automatic decision.

Do you feel inclined to help others and care for them?

Again, there can be a lot of confusion with this point. I'd like to believe in the goodness of humanity, in general. I want to think that most people feel for fellow human beings, and the people who can ignore others in pain are few and far between.

While most people feel a sense of righteousness in helping the people in need, empaths may feel a compulsory obligation to do so. Their heart is

always bleeding out for others. They may be ready to help others with complete disregard for their safety and capabilities.
The fact that they feel more deeply for the pain of other fellow beings even without being told about the problems is entirely their propriety.
Do you feel a compulsion to help others even when you know that it isn't going to be right for you?
Do you sense the pain and suffering of others and feel aggrieved?
If these emotions have been striking you left, right, and center, you can be an empath.

Do crowded places make you feel overwhelmed?

We have already discussed this point in some detail. It isn't uncommon for some people to feel overwhelmed in crowded places. However, the reason for being overwhelmed may differ in every case.
HSPs feel overwhelmed as they have high sensitivities to noise, smells, light, unwanted physical contact, and other such things. They want to get away from this discomfort at the earliest possible.
Introverts may want to avoid crowded places because they don't feel like they belong there.
However, empaths feel overwhelmed at crowded places because they are unable to control and absorb the surge of emotions they feel. In a crowded place, there would be people with no pain or sorrow. They would be radiating exuberance. It is something positive for an empath. But, at the same time, there would also be a lot of people with pain, sorrow, and sufferings entrenched deep within their hearts. An empath cannot have a filter not to absorb those emotions. It means at the same time; an empath may be getting positive and negative emotions. It can be confusing and terrifying altogether.
It is the reason most empaths feel overwhelmed in crowded places. Even if the site is not radiating mixed feelings and emotions and all the people are sad or happy simultaneously. Just think of the surge of that emotion an empath might feel because it is not the emotion of a single person but a collection.
Empaths try to avoid overcrowded places to prevent the sheer intensity of emotional assaults that happen at such sites. They are bound to feel overwhelmed with emotions if there are too many people around.
Have you ever felt that in your case?
Are crowded places too overwhelming for you?
Do you feel spent, exhausted, and drained after coming from crowded places even though you didn't interact with anyone?

Even as a child, have you always been very sensitive to the feelings and emotions of others?

It is understandable for people to become emotional as they grow because their sensitivities about pain, suffering, and emotions develop. However, as a child, our priorities are simple. As a child, up to a certain age, the survival of the self is the biggest priority.

As a child grows a little, personal happiness is the priority. A child is a happy being until a force is applied to make the child unhappy, or the child has to live in a miserable environment like extreme poverty, hunger, or terror. Even in those environments, kids find ways to entertain themselves and remain happy.

It is tough to make a child feel gloomy for very long.

However, even as a child, have you felt very sensitive to the feelings of others?

Has the pain and suffering of others besides your family members made you feel sad for very long even after it has been away from your sight?

Have you felt the 'happy' switch thrown off all of a sudden and begin to feel sad with no apparent reason?

As a child, have you experienced a switch of emotions as you might feel now?

If you answered in affirmation to these questions, you must undoubtedly probe further.

Does spending time in the lap of nature help you heal and make you feel rejuvenated?

Again, this is a contentious point, as we have discussed it earlier. Most people may feel better in the lap of nature because it is a refreshing change and provides a break from the monotony of ordinary life.

However, the reason for empaths to feel so is entirely different. The empaths do not need greenery, jungles, oceans, and hills to break the monotony, but these natural landscapes help them heal internally from the wounds of absorbing so many emotions.

Empaths absorb a lot of emotions in a day to day life and have no barriers around them. Awakened empaths can differentiate between their feelings and emotions and the ones that don't belong to them. Nevertheless, that can't prevent them from not being sad at the misery of others.

Unawakened empaths don't even have those filters. They get bombarded by a string of emotions continually and have no expertise in identification and separation. They keep feeling overwhelmed without having an experience attached to those emotions.

Now, while the empaths can absorb these emotions easily, it isn't easy to get rid of them. These feelings and emotions stick to them like leeches.

There is no medium to pass over these emotions easily. Nothing has the depth and simplicity of emotions to absorb them apart from nature.

It is a reason empaths love the lap of nature, jungles, mountains, creeks, riversides, and beaches so much. These aren't recreational places for an empath but a reservoir to submerge emotions long-held by them.

Do you feel light-hearted and healed after visiting such places?

Do you find it helpful to have lots of plants around you at your home or even at your workplace?

Do you feel a particular attachment to any specific plant?

If you answered in a yes, they might be helping you in offloading your emotions.

Have you always struggled with the idea of saying 'No' and failed miserably?

It can again be a contentious classification, but please bear with me. Many people might find it very hard to say no. However, it isn't what they say that matters but under what conditions they may say it.

Some people can't say no to others to avoid embarrassment. If you are among them, this doesn't make you an empath.

Some can't say no to their superiors, elders, parents, teachers, and bullies. The reason is fear or intimidation. They feel threatened by the consequences of replying in a 'no.' Even you can't classify such people as empaths.

However, some people can't say no because they feel that the people at the other end might get hurt or feel sad. They feel obliged to serve them and cater to their needs. They take it as their duty to cater to the needs of people in question and are ready to fulfill all the justified and unjustified demands in fear of harming them. Such people can be empaths getting exploited at the hands of narcissists and dominators or other kinds of energy vampires.

It is a fact that empaths usually have weak personal boundaries. Even the awakened empaths can fall into the traps of narcissists because they have an inherent need to cater to the needs of others and become the savior of someone in need. The narcissists are needy and opportunists that can make use of this weakness very artfully.

Have you ever felt that you have been getting exploited, and you were still unable to break free, although you knew that it was a toxic relationship?

It happens very often with empaths because, by nature, they can't see others in pain.

Do you own the feelings and emotions of others as your own?

Many empaths can make a very poor distinction between their own emotions and the emotions they absorb from others. It becomes a cause of the massive emotional overload they bear most of the time.
Awakened empaths learn to differentiate between their own emotions and the emotions that come to them from outside. They can manage their mood and emotional health better.
However, many empaths and usually unawakened empaths are unable to do so. They keep treating all emotions as their own and have to suffer a lot.
Do you always know that the emotion or feelings you are having are your own, or is there confusion at times?

Do you want to be left alone?

Many people like to live alone. There are the loners, then there are introverts, and then there are hypersensitive people. All these want to be left alone as they feel tormented in crowds. However, you can classify none of them as being an empath.
All these people want to be left alone for different reasons.
The loners have an aversion to people they don't know very well. They can mix well with the people they like. They have no problem being with people who support them emotionally and by other means. They only want to stay distant from people who might challenge them or may pose a threat by any means.
The introverts are only trying to prevent opening up to anyone. Mixing with people would mean they'd need to disclose something, and they are most afraid of doing that. Some are not confident enough to speak as they fear ridicule or embarrassment. The rest of them only want to stay confined with themselves. Their reasons for limited outreach are simple.
Hypersensitive people or HSPs don't like to mix with a lot of people as they are sensitive to noise, arguments, getting hurt, and challenged. The more they mix with people, the higher would be the risk of sensory assault. It is the reason they like to keep to themselves and prefer being left alone.
Empaths, on the other hand, want to be alone so that they can overcome the emotional overload. Empaths are necessarily not loaners. They don't fear the company of others. On the contrary, they might prefer the company of particular individuals that can help them heal.
Empaths can soak energy, feelings, and emotions from people around them. While being in a crowd may mean indiscriminate bombardment of emotions, being in the company of known individuals with positive

energy would mean absorbing positive energy. There is no reason for empaths to fear that.

Still, empaths would need a lot of alone time to get over the emotional overload they might have experienced. They can use this alone time for sitting quietly, or they can also meditate for centering their mind and grounding their energies. The ultimate purpose of this alone time is to re-energize and heal.

Do you feel better after being left alone for a while regularly?

Are you able to shake off the heaviness of the emotional burden if left alone for a while?

If that was a yes, you certainly need to probe deeply.

Do sensory inputs overstimulate you?

It is a symptom that may be shared by empaths and HSPs. Both may have an aversion to light, sound, smell, and other sensory inputs that are more intense than usual.

Although you cannot treat it as a definitive symptom of an empath, it is undoubtedly a trait that all empaths exhibit.

Intense sensory inputs overstimulate the empaths.

Does sleeping early seem like a tough job?

It may be the case with many empaths, as they usually have insomnia. Many people are night owls these days. People like to work till late. Burning the midnight oil has become a fashion in the corporate culture.

Innovators, writers, and creators like to work in the calm of the night when there are minimum sensory inputs to break their focus.

However, all of these lose their sleep for reasons utterly different than empaths.

When an innovator or creator is awake at night, there is an idea taking form in mind. Their minds are busy and highly active. That's why they resist sleep.

An empath's mind, on the other hand, might be as calm as the sea. There might not be any thought on the visible surface. However, deep down, several emotions are depriving them of sleep.

If you feel perfectly calm and yet sleep seems to ditch you for very long every night, you may need to probe further.

Have you ever felt the presence of energies and spirits you?

Now we are entering the world of speculation. The speculation is not whether there are energies or spirits or not, but whether what you feel are spirits or not.

Our mind is a fantastic make-believe machine. If you begin thinking of the presence of an entity, the brain can make it possible in your perception.

The schizophrenics won't ever believe that their world is imaginary. Everything in their world is happening for them in reality. Therefore, we are not talking about make-believe realities. Instead, we are talking about experiential realities.

There are energies, and all empaths can feel them. Irrespective of their state of wakefulness, empaths can feel energies and vibes. Most empaths use this sense to form an impression of the people they meet. They don't judge people on their external demeanor, but by the vibes they generate. Some empaths have more reliable energy reception, and they can feel the vibes more strongly than others. In the same way, some empaths can feel spirits close to them.

I used the word speculation in the beginning because, as an unawakened empath, you may not have the experiential reality to differentiate between a spirit or powerful energy and your imagination.

Therefore, you'll have to rely solely on your senses and discretion.

Have you always felt eager to do everything to keep your relationships intact?

Empaths have high people-pleasing aspirations, especially for the people they love or admire. They want to do everything in their might to keep them happy and content. They won't hesitate even to get degraded to make their loved ones happy, and this makes them prone to toxic relationships.

Although it isn't an excellent thing to have, it can be a good thing to watch out for if you want to have a classifying feature of an empath.

These are some of the things that are most common among the empaths of all types. You can try to answer all these questions honestly, and if you feel that you can fit in the description of most points, you may need an in-depth assessment.

As mentioned before, being an empath isn't good or bad but a condition. You are a person with some specific abilities and weaknesses. If you have a clear assessment of your personality, you may be able to work on your weaknesses and strengths.

It is always beneficial not only for you but also for the people associated with you. Being an awakened empath, you can be of great help to others in the form of emotional support and healing. If you have specific abilities, you can utilize them to help yourself as well as others.

PART III
EXPLORING FURTHER- GOING DEEP

CHAPTER 11
All Empaths Aren't The Same- What Kind Of An Empath Are You?

There is a general misconception that being an empath would be the same experience for everyone. There can be nothing further from the truth.

It is a fact that fundamental realities may be similar for most empaths; every empath may have a different experiential reality.

Being identified as an empath is only a distinction that helps in understanding the basic perception levels of an individual. However, not only the abilities but the trials and tribulations of each empath may differ. Empaths can have different powers based on their strengths in various segments. An empath of one type won't necessarily have capabilities of only one variety. It can be a mixture of multiple senses; some may have their core-strengths based in one faculty, while others may possess one or more. An empath doesn't get to choose these.

Nature is the ultimate enabler, and an empath is only a medium.

Therefore, it can be challenging to describe all kinds of empaths as the variations can be many. However, for the sake of better understanding, we'll discuss some of the major categories of empaths.

If you go searching on the internet, you may find information about many more types of empaths. It'd be unfair to say that those kinds of empaths are not there, but knowing those many types is only going to add to the mental clutter and help in no way. Excessive information can only cause information overload and help by no means at all. Therefore, it is always better to stick to the basics while you are still scratching the surface.

Once you have developed a thorough understanding of the concept, you can freely explore them, and you'd only find that most of the types described as different classifications are just variations of the same categories. Seeing that after you have a grip on the subject always brings clarity, whereas absorbing that information without knowing that subject would lead to mental-muck.

There are three main categories of empaths.
No matter what people tell you, there are only three main categories of empaths. The rest of them are just sub-categories or poor spin-offs.

Emotional Empaths

These are the most common empaths. It is crucial to understand that empaths aren't very common. Only 1-2 percent of people fall into this category. It runs in the genes; hence, a very high number of empaths remain confined to specific geographical locations and families.

Therefore, one is not very likely to find empaths walking on the streets wearing their empath hats for easy identification.

They are rare and difficult to spot. Even with this rarity, a very high number of empaths never really acknowledge themselves as empaths. Hence, they may be walking the streets with ordinary people without knowledge about themselves.

It shrinks the group even further. Most of the power empaths have only become apparent when an empath has realized full potential. It means that an empath can live and die without having any effect or presence felt. The only power that is usually visible and is also a symptom of being an empath is the sensitive nature of the empaths and their ability to absorb the feelings and emotions of people around them. Most empaths experience this.

Within the limited group of empaths, emotional empaths are the highest in number. It is the reason people consider all empaths as readers of feelings and emotions. There is no logical base for this presumption.

The sheer number of emotional empaths dominating the scene is so high that they have become synonymous with the whole category.

Emotional empaths are highly sensitive to the emotions and feelings of the people around them. They may inadvertently soak the feelings and emotions of people they come across and experience those feelings within themselves.

It means that if there is an emotional empath in a joyous environment, he/she may enjoy life even with several hardships because there will be a continuous inflow of positive and harmonious energy.

At the same time, if there is an emotional empath at a place where there are people in grief and sorrow, that empath will also feel the pain and sorrow with the same intensity.

The emotional empaths can feel and experience the feelings and emotions of people around them.

It is a gift and also a curse simultaneously. It is a gift because such empaths will be able to share the pure joy of the loved ones. It can become a curse as those empaths may also have to experience the pain and sorrow of every individual crossing their paths.

They may be able to console their friends better as the same pan within them. However, they may also have to feel the pain of people they may meet but may not know. Hence, while they may feel their pain, they will not have the experiences to back the pain, and the cumulative pain they might have to bear can be immense.

Awakened emotional empaths know how to handle their emotions better as they learn to distinguish between the emotions originating within their self and the ones coming from others. Once they learn to do that, it becomes easier for them not only to handle the emotional burden better but also to help the individual suffering from the emotional pain as they have genuinely experienced their pain. There can be no better person to counsel such people and set them on the right path.

Most of the time, when people go to a psychiatrist, the doctor keeps reassuring you that he/she understands the pain of the patient. However, deep down in the heart, the patient knows that the doctor might understand the illness, but there is no way to feel that pain. However, that'd not be the case with an emotional empath. This empath would have felt that pain and would be able to help in healing it collectively.

Unawakened empaths may have it tough on them as they might find it difficult to bear all that emotional overload and pain without an experiential reality.

It is similar to banging your head in a wall. When you hit your head, there is pain. However, you exactly know the cause, and although you feel the pain, there is no fear of the unknown causing the pain.

Early identification of the signs, acknowledgment of the condition, and faith in your abilities, are the three steps towards emancipation.

For help in relieving the stress of emotional overload, you can practice meditation and also talk to someone you trust.

If there are still issues, you can make use of several problem-specific remedies discussed in the second part of this book.

Physical Empaths

It is the second most widely recognized category of empaths, also known as healers. Physical empaths have the gift of tapping into the physical energies of people around them. They can not only sense the physiological issues in people around them but even feel those issues within their bodies.

Physical empaths can be very helpful in feeling chronic illnesses that keep on simmering inside the body without any symptoms for years. They can experience energy blockages as well as imbalances inside the body.

Although this may look fanciful, being a physical empath doesn't come without its trials and tribulations. When a physical empath feels some problem, the empath is also absorbing or soaking a part of that problem and experiencing it. The empath would need to develop a mechanism to cleanse their body of the absorbed energies.

Physical empaths can be amazing healers and bring great insights if they are in the field of health care. Physical healers can make a lot of difference to the lives of people around them even if they aren't specifically in health care. They may touch lives in beautiful ways on a day to day basis.

However, they'd always need to remain cautious that too much exposure to crowds can cause exhaustion, and they may take more burden that they can carry.

A physical empath can easily absorb negative energy from the people he/she interacts with, and hence excessive exposure to them can be exhaustive. It can also hurt the health of the empath. At the same time, contact with healthy and radiating people will fill the empath with positive energy. If the empath can somehow maintain a balance, it'd work wonders.

Exercise, healthy food, and meditation can help a physical empath in radiating positive energy to more and more people.

Intuitive Empaths

The remaining types of empaths that you may have heard of belong with this category and the branches that follow.

It is vital to understand that the human mind has unlimited potential. All the other empath abilities that people have are related to the brain and its infinite power. Therefore, you can put them under one header for the ease of understanding.

An intuitive empath will have better clarity of thought and perception. Such an individual will be able to not only sense the feelings and emotions of a person but might also be able to understand that person with greater clarity. Such empaths have a clearer understanding of dreams and may also be able to perceive the dangers of the future much before they take place.

They may sense the energies and emotions of even plants and animals. Several animals can sense natural disasters much before they take place. Even the high-tech scientific instruments are not able to predict earthquakes and tsunamis as some animals can. In the same way, some empaths who are in tune with the earth can sense such dangers before they occur.

Intuitive empaths can have these sorts of mental abilities.

Some of the notable intuitive empath categories are:

Dream Empaths

Most of us dream almost every night, but very few people can remember those dreams. Whatever information people retain, they are unable to make out anything significant from those dreams.

That's not the limitation for dream empaths. They are avid dreamers, and they can not only have vivid dreams but may also be able to deduce useful and intuitive information from those dreams. Such empaths can also help other people in deciphering their dreams.

Dream empaths can get insightful cues from their dreams that can help in several meaningful ways.

These people can especially heal people carrying painful baggage from their past that has been making their lives challenging. They can help such individuals in understanding the meaning of their dreams and the things that they need to resolve to move ahead in their lives. It might look like the job of a shrink, but it is crucial to understand that a psychiatrist may have limitations of information that the individual may not be in a position to explain. A dream empath may not have such restrictions due to the intuitive abilities at disposal.

Precognitive Empaths

Most people understand precognition, as this is a term very commonly used in the movies. It might look like a part of the fiction, but some empaths may be able to see the future much before it happens.

There will be critics, but one must understand how energy works. We all have a consciousness that is just a part of the integrated awareness of this universe. At one level, everything has emerged from oneness. Therefore, our sense of awareness or subconscious can establish a connection with the larger consciousness.

Déjà vu is a phenomenon that sounds believable. Having intuition that you might have witnessed the events that happened just now much before is believable. Even ordinary people have had this experience several times. All this can only be possible if there is a force that can help us see those things.

Ordinary people have limited abilities to have such visions, while precognitive empaths can establish a much better link. It helps them see future events with greater clarity and consistency.

Telepathic Empaths

Telepathy is the ability to communicate with others intuitively and carry out an exchange of information. Many characters in popular TV programs owned such powers, and people felt fascinated by them. That was a time before the invention of mobile phone technology.

Nevertheless, even in this age, owning a power where you can penetrate the mind of someone else and know the real secrets can be invaluable.

Although telepathy doesn't work exactly like this, you get the framework. An empath having telepathic powers will be able to read the minds of others and connect with them intuitively.

Psychometric Empaths

These are the empaths who can receive some cue even from inanimate objects like jewelry, photographs, and personal possessions.

Some empaths can get the vibes of a person and also their emotional state from their personal belongings.

Mediumship Empaths

These empaths have a deeper connection with energies, and they can feel the presence of all kinds of energies around them.

No matter how much science tries to deny the presence of spirits, ghosts, and energies, it wouldn't change the fact that some people do feel the presence of these entities around them.

Those that can't understand their presence and motives might feel scared. Mediumship empaths have a deeper connection with energies, and hence they can communicate with and understand them better.

Such empaths act as the bridge between the spirits on the other side and this world.

Earth Empaths

These empaths have a deeper connection with the earth and all the changes happening inside it. They are in a better position to predict any sudden natural calamity or change.

These empaths feel deeply connected with the energies of the earth and therefore find it very easy to understand the changes in advance.

Plant Empaths

These empaths have a deep connection with their plants and may be able to understand their needs better. Such empaths can be very helpful for farmers as they can predict problems with crops and suggest ways to improve the harvest.

They may also be able to predict monsoon and drought more accurately.

Animal Empaths

These empaths can feel for the animals around them. They may be able to befriend animals easily and understand their needs. Such empaths can be very helpful in understanding their problems and provide a fitting solution based on their assessments.

CHAPTER 12
What Difference Does Being An Empath Have On Life?

The answer to this question will have two parts:
First, the impact of being an empath on you
Second, the impact of you being an empath for the world
We'll deal with both the aspects sequentially so that there is clarity on this question as it may arise in your life at several points.
Being an empath isn't an easy road. There would be many instances when you will have serious doubts about yourself, and you may want to believe that there is no such thing as an empath, or there is no merit in being so. An understanding of this question will help you in being determined on your path.

First, the impact of being an empath on you

It is the most important one of the two, and hence you must pay close attention.
Being an empath will always be a reality for you. It will never be a choice but a truth. Now there are two ways to deal with this reality.
First, you can acknowledge and accept the reality irrespective of the fact that you like it or not and begin working on modifying it as per your needs. It is always a better and more sensible way of dealing with reality.
Second, you may choose to live in denial for as long as you can wish or afford. It isn't a natural way, but many people still want to ignore reality and live in denial. They'll have to live with the consequences of being an unawakened empath. It means that they'll have weak boundaries or inferior filters to prevent getting affected by the oncoming emotions and feelings. They will not be able to distinguish between their feelings and emotions and the ones they absorb from the environment. They may suffer mood swings, depression, and severe anxieties, and these can worsen with time. They might experience all these and much more, but will not be able to experience the abilities that come along with them. They won't be able to develop the skills because they'd never acknowledge and accept their gift and have faith in it.
Most people are empaths by birth. It is just like having your limbs or other sensory organs, and there is no reason to run away from these.
Not recognizing that you are an empath can have a debilitating effect on your life as leading a healthy life may become very challenging. You may experience the rush of emotions that others don't.
However, it will always be up to you to recognize your gift and embrace it with the confidence and respect it deserves.

Second, the impact of you being an empath for the world

As an empath, you must understand that the world may benefit from your gift if you can polish it and use it for the benefit of others. You may get praise and lots of good wishes. You can do a lot of good to others by using your gift as we have discussed in the previous chapter the things empaths can do and the way those can make a difference to the world.

However, if you don't accept your gift or choose to ignore it, the world may never care. It will be more of an internal struggle for you, and the world can ridicule you for that but not sympathize.

Being an empath may not have been your decision, but it is a responsibility thrust upon you. We all come with specific responsibilities in this world. Some people succeed remarkably, and the world acknowledges, respects, and adores them. But, the unfortunate ones that are unable to fulfill their respective responsibilities are either ridiculed or forgotten without a mention.

It will always be up to you to make of the opportunity that has come in front of you.

CHAPTER 13
The Thin Line Of Being An Empath

We have discussed at length the potential an empath has. There is no doubt that if you are an unawakened empath, you will have an opportunity to become much more than you think you already are. There is a road that goes towards greatness or at least purposefulness. You can make your life more objective and goal-oriented, where you can reach out to more and more people and help them.

However, every path that goes towards greatness will also have a diversion at some point towards destructiveness.

Undoubtedly, empaths have a potential for greatness, but they also have an equal amount of potential for hara-kiri or self-destruction.

An empath who has such a great desire to serve others can quickly turn into a narcissist who would know nothing but to exploit.

Empaths and narcissists are two different personalities. However, they have a high affinity towards each other. If an empath doesn't get hold of the faculties and channelize them in the correct direction, the feeling of victimhood and entitlement may sweep in swiftly and silently.

An unawakened and immature empath may begin to undermine the need to earn and may start thinking that he/she deserves attention and the perks that come along.

If the thin line is blurred, then the tables might turn from the need to serve others to a sense of entitlement. It can be the first step towards narcissism.

The whole discourse for the empath may change from being independent, responsible, and self-reliant to dependency, getting served, and taken care of by others.

It doesn't take much of an effort to become a parasite from a benefactor.

With Great Power Comes Great Responsibility

These words from the movie spiderman hold great significance in the context of empaths.

You don't choose to become an empath. It is a selection made by nature. But because you are the chosen one, it is your responsibility to take it forward.

Even a beautiful rose comes with thorns. There is no success without challenges.

It is the responsibility of an empath to rise over brooding and make the best of the opportunities at hand.

CHAPTER 14
Beware Of The Things That Can Take You Down

An empath is a positive force. It is the reason an empath has to bear so many hardships. You are the beacon of positive energy who can redirect others in the right direction.

However, does that mean you won't face challenges? On the contrary, you may have to face many more hardships than the people you may guide.

In this world, the struggle between the good and the bad is eternal. The good can only win if it keeps reinforcing itself and doesn't allow weaknesses to penetrate its borders.

As an empath, it will be imperative for you to stay away from influences that can weaken you or subdued your powers. It isn't going to be easy anyway, but it'll become a lot harder if you give in to habits that are eroding in nature.

Your habits must help you in preserving your positive energy and keep your aura intact.

Emotionally, empaths can be under a lot of pressure most of the time. Giving way to emotional weaknesses can be very damaging.

An empath also needs to stay on guard all the time as negative energies are continually trying to take charge in various forms. They can come in the way of being too proud or looking for too much praise.

Therefore, it is the responsibility of an empath to adopt habits that keep detrimental influences away.

Preventing Negative Influence

Don't Try to Become a People Pleaser: When you are doing something beneficial for others, the desire to hear some praise is natural. Once in a while, you may get appreciation, and there will be times when you'll do what you do and move on without waiting for the praise. An empath should ideally function in this way. However, empaths are generally hungry for love and admiration. They do not care much about the ones that are usually grateful but desire the appreciation of the hard ones to please.

More often than not, the hard ones to please are narcissists that exploit this weakness of empaths. You'd keep trying to please them, and they'll keep exhausting you and draining you of the energy.

The empaths must believe in the true principles of 'Karma.' You only have the action in your hand, and the result should not be your concern. If you are deserving, you will get the result.

If you follow this principle in life, you will face less burden, and there will be much less emotional load on your heart.

You must understand that you do not have the responsibility to please a specific individual. Your reach can be extensive, and you must be useful for many rather than the ones you desire to please.

Do not Try to Carry People Over Your Shoulders: There is a beautiful quote,

> Give a man a fish, and you feed him for a day.
> Teach a man to fish, and you feed him for a lifetime.

It is a priceless lesson empaths need to learn. Many empaths begin trying to carry others over their shoulders. The people they are bearing become parasites as they understand that as long as they don't do anything, you'll fend for them.

It is going to drain you of your positive energy, and you'll begin losing the steam. You neither need to bear others nor need to ignore their misdeeds. The more you allow people to exploit you, the heavier they'll get.

Stop Being a Sacrificial Lamb for Others: Sacrificial attitude is a common occurrence in empaths. They'd not hesitate to take the blame of others onto their heads. Even when they know that they haven't committed a mistake, they may take the responsibility to save others. It may seem as if they have made a moral high ground, but they are digging a pit for themselves as well as for the people they were trying to save.

When they take the blame for the mistakes committed by others, they are effectively sending a message that there is always a way to escape after doing anything wrong. Crime and punishment should be proportional. When they don't get punished, they can become even more irresponsible. Even the empaths won't go unscathed.

If they keep owning the mistakes of others so rampantly, the burden they might have to carry can get crushing.

Using Victimhood as a Tool: This isn't something that most empaths do, but the ones that try to become a messiah of others may want to play this card. Once in a while, you can feel like a victim. However, you can't keep playing the victim card for too long. Once you get addicted to the sympathies and attention you get being a victim, you'd find it very difficult to get on your feet.

Most empaths have the ultimate desire for love and attention. The victimhood card may help them get both very easily, and they might feel compelled to play that card all too long, which can be dangerous. It can get them out of sync of their energies.

Permitting Others to Take You for Granted: Being forgiving is a virtue that most people don't possess. It is a rarity. However, you can't be so forgiving that people begin treating you as a punching bag or a doormat.

Getting trampled too often is a weakness and not a virtue.

An empath may have just one desire that is to serve others and cater to the needs of the ones that need their attention. However, this also has the potential to become a weakness very quickly.

You may have the desire to serve at the core of your heart, but you can't allow that to become a 'Kick Me' sign on your back.

An empath must develop the diligence to understand when someone is taking undue advantage of him/her because it may happen very often.

Not Conserving Your Energy: Energy will always remain a crucial issue. An empath can optimally function only when there is abundant energy. Empaths can begin losing power quickly. Several things may make an empath feel the emotional, mental, or physical drain.

If you allow your energies to get wasted on petty and useless things and people, you may not be able to pay attention to the real needy. If you are not able to help a needy, that will put an additional load of guilt on you. You must ensure that you aren't wasting your energy on useless people and objectives.

You must choose your priorities judiciously and remain clear of your objectives.

Preventing Emotional Burnout

In this world, nothing is endless. You can exhaust anything if you get on to it. Many empaths like to live in the sweet misconception that they have infinite love and affection to give. Little do they know that their ability to deliver is limited even more.

Emotional, physical, and mental burnout is the usual malice that affects empaths. Irrespective of the cognitive development and firm boundaries, it isn't possible to prevent total burnout. Empaths are sensitive beings, and they can't help but absorb the pain and suffering of others. There's nothing much they can do about it anyway.

However, it can be dreadful if an empath consciously begins attracting that drain upon himself or herself for long. The inability to say no to others and inadequate understanding of the limits is a common cause of the problem.

No matter the cause, if there is an emotional burnout, not only the empath but also the people around them would suffer.

There are several ways an empath can prevent the burnout:

Find the Healing Time: Every empath needs time to heal. It is the crucial me-time that empaths can utilize to ward off the excessive emotions and re-energize. At times, the empaths become so addicted to the appreciation and adoration they are getting that they stop paying attention to the emotional overload that can cause burnout.

Catering to the needs of others is a fantastic feat, but an empath must find alone time now and then to heal internally. Excessive load can affect an empath's ability to reach out to others through the energy field.

Decrease Attachment Dependency: Empaths are prone to attachments. They may keep denying the fact, but they want to cling on to the select few they love and adore. It can easily lead to dependencies that can hamper emotional and spiritual development.

They may become focused only on a few people and stop paying attention to the larger goals. It can also make them even more sensitive as their emotional focus would remain centered around a select few, and they would begin regulating the emotions authoritatively.

All this would eventually cause emotional burnout. More often than not, such relationships become toxic, and the empath begins to get dominated.

If an empath wants to prevent this, becoming dependent on a select few for all your emotional needs can be dangerous. An empath must try to find an alternate way to release pressure and heal. Meditation, exercise, and work can be the other areas that can also help an empath gain more emotional liberation.

Boundaries: Ineffective personal boundaries are the definitive cause of emotional burnouts in empaths. It is a widely recognized fact. The weaker the own boundaries an empath has, the poor will be the regulation of emotions that affect the empath from outside.

An empath must have firm boundaries to prevent excessive and overreaching assault on his/her emotional capacity.

Many a time, empaths give unhindered access to themselves to others. They become the oasis from which people can draw out anything anytime. There can be no way to sustain this behavior.

An empath must understand the limitations and also maintain a breather space.

An empath must also understand that there is a significant difference in feeling with someone and feeling for someone. One cannot own the emotions of others indiscriminately and survive unhindered.

Your heart may reach out for others, but you must set limits to the extent you can go. If you begin feeling for everyone around you, your system will be unable to hold it.

Effective boundaries are a must for the smooth functioning of an empath.

Try to Become Impersonal: It is the nature of an empath to begin to feel as others are feeling. However, empaths must understand that there is an extent to which they can keep doing so effectively.

If you begin feeling rage, apathy, hatred, and other such feelings within you, it won't take long for you to feel exhausted.

You will have to learn to become impersonal. While you can understand the emotions of people around you much better than anyone else, it'd be immature to begin to feel all the feelings within yourself. It can lead to emotional burnout very quickly.

Get Out of Savior Mode: This is another major issue that becomes a cause of emotional burnouts. Empaths make it their mission to save the lost causes. They must understand that they can't rescue those that don't want to in the state they are. They are likely even to drag you in their world as they act as swamps. The harder you try, the deeper you get.

As an empath, it isn't your duty to save the world. You can become a medium to help others through your skills, but you should drop the idea of trying to rescue the lost causes.

You must understand that they are eventually going to get submerged in their acts, and you are going to get repentance that will lead to emotional burnout.

Preventing emotional burnout is a must for an empath because if that begins to happen often, the empath may start to get drawn towards addictions to heal the pain and numb the sensations. It is a destruction path for any empath, and most walk down this road because they overestimate their abilities and then try to over utilize them.

An empath must respect the limits and always try to prevent negative influences on the personality and emotional burnouts as they can cause irreparable damage in the long run.

CHAPTER 15
Learning To Be An Empath With Confidence

No matter what you are, it is crucial to embrace it fully with confidence if you want to get anywhere. Being an empath can be no exception. There can be absolutely no doubt that the road to realizing your powers can be a bit bumpy.

An empath may not have it easy as several impediments come from your self-doubt. It is comparatively easy to tackle practical challenges as they are open and direct. However, when you get challenged from within, the fight gets tough.

But, you must understand that you don't have a way out. Being an empath isn't a religion that you can renounce or which you can stop practicing; it is an attribute.

The faster you accept your realities, acknowledge the challenges in front, and develop faith in your abilities, the sooner you'll be able to get hold of your faculties and life.

Several practices can help an empath in strengthening positive attributes. It would help if you did not only work on reinforcing your positive attributes but also worked on effective protection strategies and grounding techniques.

Reinforcing Positive Attributes

Develop Faith: Here, the word faith implies 'trust and confidence.' You can be a believer of any religion, or may not believe in any. It is inconsequential for an empath. Being an empath has nothing much to do with religion. You can very well be a believer, an atheist, or an agnostic, and it may all be the same for you. The most important thing that would determine the outcome for you would be your faith in your abilities.

Most people live in utter disbelief of their abilities all their lives, and sure enough, the skills evade them mercilessly. You must have complete trust in your abilities to make them work. It is the leap of faith you would have to take.

The only way out for an empath is to have complete trust in the abilities and continually work on refining them. It is like sharpening the ax. The sharper the tool, the shorter it'll take to cut down the tree.

Try Emotional Detachment: I know we have discussed this term in the previous chapter, but believe me, this is the biggest entrapment for most empaths. The stronger the emotional attachment you have, the easier it'd take for someone else to flip the switch for you.

As an empath, you must understand that the higher the potential for going up, the stronger is the attraction to look down and quiver.

Try to be as emotionally independent as you can. There is no harm in having more robust relationships and love, as they are the must. The problem begins when empaths begin to rely on those relationships for all their needs and lose their identity.

Meditate: Nothing can be more helpful for an empath to meditate regularly. Meditation is the most refreshing act that an empath would experience. It helps in grounding the energies and also unloading the emotional baggage you have been carrying.

It doesn't take much to meditate. You can do it practically anywhere, anytime. However, it'd be best if empaths can have a fixed time to meditate every day as that helps them in recharging themselves once a day, at least. If you aren't very particular about anything, it is easy to miss it in the veil of excuses.

Practice Release Regularly: It is another must for empaths. They hoard all types of energies within them as they are walking sponges of energies, emotions, and feelings. These can weigh them down and have a toll not only on their personality but also on their functioning.

They should try to release as much energy as possible through activities like running, shouting, screaming, and high-intensity workouts. The more spent force they can release, the lighter they'll feel.

Practice Mindfulness: Being mindful is a way of life. It is a technique that helps you remain grounded in realities, and you can easily pull yourself back from the emotional and mental entrapments.

It is a straightforward technique of living in the moment and experiencing every phenomenon with complete immersion. It can prevent empaths from falling in the trap of emotions, feelings, and experiences that do not belong to them.

An empath can easily ward off anxieties, stress, and negative emotions by being mindful of the current situation. It is no magic. On the contrary, mindfulness can help us break the spell of imaginary struggles that we create, causing stress and anxieties.

It is a technique that helps us in identifying reality with greater clarity.

Grounding Techniques

It is common for empaths to lose their ground or begin feeling out of sync. It often happens when the empath feels a rush of emotions or gets overwhelmed. It can create a feeling of detachment, disillusionment, and loss of connection.

It might happen very often with an empath due to high sensitivities. The good news is that such things aren't permanent. You can quickly get over such feelings by grounding yourself.

Some Easy Grounding Techniques are:
Aligning Your Root Chakra: The root chakra or the base chakra, also known as the Mooladhara, helps us establish connections with the mother earth. It allows all the negative energies built up inside us to seep into the ground and facilitates fresh energy restoration.

You can practice root chakra meditations, and you'll find that grounding the senses would become very easy. Root chakra meditation also helps us in strengthening our energies and building determination. If you have been struggling with self-doubt and self-determination, this chakra meditation can be of immense help.

Tree Exercise: Trees are the best example of benevolence, forgiveness, and tolerance. They are stable, reliable, and determined. An empath can draw a lot of positive energy from a tree and also unload a lot of negative emotions. Hugging a tree can help you transfer all the negative energy that can pass on from the tree to the ground.

Even sitting under a big tree can help you feel grounded.

Drumming: Drumming loudly and passionately can also help you feel more grounded—the vibrations arising from drumming help in settling the dust of emotions within you. It enables you to feel at ease, and you'll find your stress melting away after a session.

Using Essential Oils: Essential oils are also helpful in calming your senses. They have a very soothing effect on the energy chakras and also help in rebalancing your chakras. There are several ways in which you can use essential oils. However, empaths may follow caution when dealing with specific essential oils as they can even make you more excitable and overwhelmed.

Healthy Diet: Our food has a powerful impact on our personality and the way we function. People relying too much on hot and spicy foods are more likely to have a fiery temperament and emotional makeup. An empath needs to be stable and must retain energy for long as there is constant energy loss. A diet that comprises of root vegetables, nuts, and other energy-rich foods can help an empath in remaining grounded.

These are just some of the methods that can help you in feeling grounded, and you'll be able to function as an empath better.

CONCLUSION

Thank you for making it through to the end of this book; let's hope it was informative and able to provide you with all of the tools you need to achieve your goals, whatever they may be.

The purpose of this book was to clear the air about empaths and deal with the popular myths and misconceptions about them. Empaths are not fictional characters but a reality. However, they can be completely different from what people popularly consider them to be.

The objective of this book was to explain what it means to be an empath, and the kind of struggles an empath has to undergo. There is not much clarity about the trials and tribulations of empaths as the world only likes to know the fascinating things.

This book has tried to explain the real lives of empaths and the things they need to do to realize their powers and feel connected to the mainstream.

It is a painful thing that an empath who has an immense potential may spend the whole life cursing the characteristics that are a gift. Many empaths not only perish in oblivion but have to bear a painful existence because they are never able to learn to live with their condition.

The popular fiction either finds interest in lionizing their image or belittling them. This book has tried to present a realistic representation of empaths and the things empaths need to understand to become a fruitful part of the mainstream world.

However, it is still solving half the problem. This book would help you in understanding the complexities of being an empath and various aspects of it.

You would have come to know by now that empaths have to bear a lot of pain and trauma. Their lives cannot be as simple as ordinary people. Therefore, empaths need healing and support regularly.

If they do not get healing, they can become a dumping ground of emotions.

The second part of this book would help you understand various ways to carry out Empath Healing.

It would give you a detailed account of all the healing strategies and how empaths can enforce their energy fields.

I hope that you will be able to gain full advantage of the information provided by this book.

Finally, if you enjoyed this book, please let me know your thoughts with a short review on Amazon. It means a lot, thank you!

DESCRIPTION

Learn to Identify the Signs That Can Unlock the Doors of Mystical Powers Within You

Have you ever felt that your intuition warned you better than others in specific scenarios?

Has it ever occurred that you felt you had seen an event happening much before it took place?

Have you had bad feelings about something wrong about to happen?

Have you felt that others don't understand you fully?

If you've had such doubts before and never had an answer to those, this book is your chance. **Read More**

Do you feel that you are emotionally very volatile and have severe mood swings?

Do you think you can feel the feelings and emotions of others better?

Do you feel like a misfit as others are unable to understand you?

Do you feel unloved and drawn to people that seem to be narcissists?

Do you have an aversion to sensory inputs like bright lights and loud noises?

Does venturing out in crowded places seem to drain and exhaust you?

Did you know if you exhibit some of these symptoms, you may be an empath?

Pop culture has portrayed empaths is a very incorrect light. They have lionized the characters to the extent that they seem to be unbelievable. It sounds as if they can't exist. But, did you know that almost 1-2 percent of people in this world are empaths?

Did you know that most empaths keep struggling with emotional overload all their lives?

Did you know empaths may begin feeling exhausted as soon as they pass through crowds?

Do you know being an empath looks like a curse to most empaths, and it is more likely to stay that way for them?

Did you know that an empath doesn't need to live like that because there are ways to get over all kinds of empath fatigue?

If you want to know the ways to get over empath fatigue and get healing, **Read More**

Being an empath is an opportunity that can enable you to help others and live a more fulfilling life. However, some empaths are never able to capitalize on the opportunity due to their ignorance about empath healing.

If you want to know the real truth about empaths and the possibilities they have, and the ways to address issues that might come on the way, **Read More**

In this Book, You Will Find:
- Comprehensive understanding of empaths
- Explanation of fear and enigma behind empaths
- Understand, whether it is a boon or a bane?
- Learn why most empaths are never able to realize their potential
- Disadvantages of being an unawakened empath
- The things you can accomplish being an awakened empath
- The things that you'd need to do
- The reason people easily exploit empaths
- Why empaths fail to have stable relationships despite their caring nature
- The struggles in the life of unawakened empaths
- Characteristic traits of an empath
- Signs to look for
- Things it means to be an empath
- Different kinds of empaths
- The ways to prevent degradation of power
- Steps to reinforce the power

And Much More....

EMPATH HEALING

Beginner's Guide to Improve Your Empathy Skills, Increase Self-Esteem, Protect Yourself From Energy Vampires, and Overcome Fears With Emotional Intelligence

Valery Blake

© Copyright 2020 by Valery Blake. All right reserved.

The work contained herein has been produced with the intent to provide relevant knowledge and information on the topic on the topic described in the title for entertainment purposes only. While the author has gone to every extent to furnish up to date and true information, no claims can be made as to its accuracy or validity as the author has made no claims to be an expert on this topic. Notwithstanding, the reader is asked to do their own research and consult any subject matter experts they deem necessary to ensure the quality and accuracy of the material presented herein.

This statement is legally binding as deemed by the Committee of Publishers Association and the American Bar Association for the territory of the United States. Other jurisdictions may apply their own legal statutes. Any reproduction, transmission or copying of this material contained in this work without the express written consent of the copyright holder shall be deemed as a copyright violation as per the current legislation in force on the date of publishing and subsequent time thereafter. All additional works derived from this material may be claimed by the holder of this copyright.

The data, depictions, events, descriptions and all other information forthwith are considered to be true, fair and accurate unless the work is expressly described as a work of fiction. Regardless of the nature of this work, the Publisher is exempt from any responsibility of actions taken by the reader in conjunction with this work. The Publisher acknowledges that the reader acts of their own accord and releases the author and Publisher of any responsibility for the observance of tips, advice, counsel, strategies and techniques that may be offered in this volume.

INTRODUCTION

Empaths can be the feelers and healers in this world full of insensitivities. A world where most people never have the time to think beyond themselves, empaths have a heart open for everyone. They have the potential to not only feel the pain of others but also to help in it. Yet most remain constrained to fighting their struggles, and a majority of them don't win. This book will help you understand how empath healing can become a potent tool to empower you as an empath to work for the betterment of others without compromising your happiness and peace.

Congratulations on purchasing this book, and thank you for doing so.

Empath healing is essential for any empath to function effectively in public, as well as personal life. However, it remains mostly ignored due to a lack of knowledge and awareness.

Most empaths are either fully aware of their state or busy struggling with the issues in their simple ways. The result is usually not good because they end up secluding themselves or giving in to various addictions.

Empath healing can help all empaths get over their emotional overload, problems in dealing with relationships, utilization of their gifts, and other such shortcomings.

In this book, I have discussed various aspects of empath healing that can help you in dealing with such issues.

From difficulties in overcoming challenges like overcoming overwhelming emotions to facing large gatherings and crowds, this book has discussed every aspect of emotional overloading in detail.

This book will also help you understand the various stages of evolution of an empath and how you can use this information to stay motivated. This book will help you in looking at it with a positive perspective and not entirely as a challenge.

This book is a comprehensive document designed to help you with emotional triggers, relationship challenges, stress, fatigue, and exhaustion all caused due to over absorption of emotions.

It will not only tell you the ways but guide you in a step by step manner in practicing those methods effectively.

From tools for personal growth to meditation and grounding techniques, this book has given every aspect its due space.

This book is straightforward and easy to understand so that everyone can take advantage of this information.

I hope that you will be able to get the full advantage of this book.

There are plenty of books on this subject on the market; thanks again for choosing this one! I have made every effort to ensure it is full of as much useful information as possible; please enjoy it!

CHAPTER 1
Empath Healing- Why Is It Needed?

Being an empath can be challenging. Consider the challenges of being different in a homogenous world. It is easy to begin feeling lonely and alienated. It can cause a lot of stress and anxiety.

Empaths are also highly sensitive individuals and get stimulated relatively faster. Irrespective of the fact whether it is an awakened or unawakened empath, the absorption of energies, feelings, and emotion is very high. It can also begin taking a toll on the health and overall performance of the empaths.

Therefore, it is not uncommon that, more often than not, many empaths find themselves restless, anxious, drained, and disillusioned. Most empaths find it difficult even to cope up with the day to day activities as effortlessly as other people in their surroundings can do.

Empaths are different. There are many things in which empaths are more potent than others. They are more sensitive, and they also have higher intuitive abilities. Empaths can do several things that many people can't even dream of and aspire to do. In a nutshell, empaths are more complex and capable than others.

However, you also can't ignore the fact that the more complex and powerful a machine is, the more downtime it'll face. The same is the case with empaths.

Their high sensitivities and porous nature, coupled with their inability to mix with people like others and have an ordinary life, can easily have a profound impact on their performance and behavior.

It makes empath healing a vital subject whose importance every empath must understand.

Unfortunately, it is a fact that a very high percentage of empaths don't even acknowledge or realize what they are. The minute portion of empaths that have recognized their state and realized their powers tend to overuse them. All these can lead to several issues that may cause severe degradation in their day to day functioning as well as have a profound impact on their mental health.

As I have already mentioned and you may have the realization that being an empath isn't easy. It is a path on which you have to walk alone. There may be minimal support and understanding that you may get from others, and there are several struggles that you face every waking moment of your life.

These can leave you feeling exasperated, drained, sad, and lonely. All this makes empath healing all the more critical.

Some of the things that you might experience in your everyday lives are:

Why You May Be in Urgent Need of Empath Healing

Waking Up Exhausted In the Morning

It is one of the most common problems that empaths usually face. Sleeping on time is always a challenging task for empaths. It has nothing to do with the fact that you are an awakened empath or the one unbeknownst of your state. A lot is always simmering in the conscious and subconscious mind of an empath. Having control over thoughts or disassociating from them can be challenging. That is a reason sleep is always playing hide and seek.

Mental calm is the first requirement for a night of sound sleep, and that is a tough thing for an empath. Even smaller incidents have such a profound impact on the minds of empaths that calm is always elusive. It is something only an empath can understand, and the rest of the world never be able to come to terms with it.

A cloudy mind can also lead to anxieties and restlessness even while you are sleeping. Even as a result of this, you might wake up feeling exhausted in the morning.

In general, it has become a fashion to brag about being a night owl. People like to party all night, and yet they don't feel that kind of strain and exhaustion in the morning. The reason is simple. While they might be bearing physical exhaustion, their minds aren't full of stress, anxiety, and negative emotions. They can make up for the loss of sleep with a few hours of sound sleep.

At the same time, an empath may keep tossing and turning in the bed without an iota of sleep in the eyes. There is always a storm of thoughts in mind.

As I said, this is a common problem in empaths of all kinds, and it isn't a problem you can take lightly. It can affect your performance in personal as well as professional lives.

Empath healing can help you in settling the storm of clouds in your mind, and you can have the rest that helps you in waking up energetic in the morning.

With the help of empathic healing, you'll not only be able to feel energetic, but there will also be higher productivity and positivity. You'll not get burdened by any challenge coming your way and will have the energy to face the challenges with an open mind.

A Nagging Fear of Something Amiss

It is a problem particular to empaths. The biggest drawback of being highly intuitive is that it can get hard to quell fears that may not have a form yet.

Almost every empath would agree to the fact that there have been times they seriously felt that something wrong was about to happen. As an empath, you can't ignore such fears. You have high intuitive powers, and such feelings usually have a meaning.

However, most empaths fail to come to terms with the fact that the nagging fear of something wrong about to happen can be due to several other reasons.

- Most empaths tend to overthink things. Even in general, if you begin to overthink something, the mind would ultimately divert you towards a depressing or fearful conclusion. It is a part of the survival instinct that has made us draw the worst-case scenarios in everything. The more you live in your mind, the higher would be the chances of reaching fearful conclusions. The problem with empaths is that they are living in their minds most of the time, and that's why there can be nagging fears of something wrong about to happen when there is no real danger nearby.
- The body needs to be in a rested and calm state to have positive thoughts. However, as we have discussed this even in the previous point, calm and sleep are usually evasive of empaths. Exhaustion and exasperation can also lead to fear and anxious thoughts that can fill an empath with fear and dread.
- Empaths need very high energy levels within themselves to work efficiently. Nobody loses energy faster than an empath. If an empath isn't getting enough rest and sleep, there will be no replenishment of energy. Fear and dread can also lead to negative energy. In such a case, if an empath finds himself/herself crowded by negative people, it can make an empath less enthusiastic about helping people around. This lack of enthusiasm can also lead to the nagging fear of something going amiss.

Irrespective of the cause, this is a sign that the energy levels in the empath are diminishing. Empath healing becomes a must for an empath in such a scenario.

You must also understand that there will be no formal communication to you about healing from within. It is something that you must recognize. Every empath may have different healing needs. Someone living and working in a stressful environment may need healing frequently; at the same time, an empath living in seclusion or a monetary may not need healing very often.

Unreasonable fears are signs that something is going amiss. As an empath, you must acknowledge these signs and pay attention to your energy healing.

Having Mind Fog or Episodes of Absent Mindedness

It is another significant sign that every empath must never ignore. You can accuse an empath of several things, but lack of attention to something is not one among them for sure. Empaths are not only attentive to things they can see but also to things they can't.

However, there will be times when an empath would find it excessively difficult to focus on things. There would be a lot of mental fog. You'd find yourself lost in thought even when people are talking to you or vying for your attention. You may find it increasingly hard to focus on current issues, and your mind will begin to remain engaged in thoughts you may not recognize.

In this condition, you may also begin to feel out of sync with the things currently taking place. It isn't a hypothetical scenario but some of the most common things that an empath experiences in everyday life.

High sensitivities, better cognitive abilities, and intuitiveness are the trademarks of most empaths. Mental fog and absent-mindedness are clear signs that an empath is struggling with calm and balance.

Empath healing is a must in such circumstances. Healing for an empath is not a luxury or treat but a necessity. Without recovery, an empath may begin to feel drained, exhausted, and unenthusiastic. It may also push an empath to seek other methods of numbing pain and stress. Addictions become a real possibility for empaths in such circumstances.

Increasing Annoyance From People Around

An empath is a person who has a weeping heart for everyone. An empath will heal anyone who comes near. There is an indiscriminate distribution of positive energy to the people in the vicinity. However, you can't help but feel annoyed when you begin to get a sense that people around you are an excessive drain on your energy levels. The people who don't need your positive energy, but they are filling you up with negative energy leading to faster depletion of your energy levels.

It happens with empaths very often in competitive work environments with a lot of toxic people around. You may even experience that when you are among friends and acquaintances with negative energies.

Such people keep on exciting and stimulating empaths, and massive energy loss takes place. It can have a profound impact on the general character and attitude of an empath.

An empath has a general character of helping people around. However, the excessive influence of such people may lead to a false sense of disillusionment and apathy towards others, in general.

An empath may begin to feel surrounded by such people and may start to avoid helping others. In reality, an empath may not be in a position to help. Such people can drain all positive energy.

Empath healing is the only way empaths can begin to feel normal.

You must understand that helping others isn't a choice for an empath but a part of the character. If the state of annoyance continues for long, it can push empaths towards additions.

Frequent Emotional Outbursts

It isn't uncommon for empaths to feel sorrow, pain, and grief of others. However, they also have a mechanism to let these emotions pass away. They aren't strangers to the phenomenon of emotions sweeping over them out of the blue like a bolt of lightning. But, over time, empaths get used to such instances and develop some endurance.

However, if you have started feeling stressed, anxious, and overwhelmed all too often and a bit too much, it can be a cause of concern. If you have begun to break down too often and there are instances when you start to cry in public or become angry out of the blue, you must become cautious. These are signs of low energy levels. You will need energy healing immediately.

Public emotional outbursts for empaths is not a regular occurrence. If that has begun to take place all too very often, you must seek empath healing for the replenishment of your energy levels. Centering the mind and grounding yourself is very important in such circumstances.

Empath healing doesn't take much effort, and it is a necessity. An empath, irrespective of his/her role in society, cannot ignore empath healing because it is crucial not only for keeping them productive but also to prevent them from turning toxic for the community.

The Feeling of Loneliness and Alienation

It can also begin to happen with empaths. Empaths never feel at home to a great extent. They are living in a world of 8 billion people, and yet they find very few like them. Empaths quickly begin to feel like misfits when they can't do simple things and adopt typical behavior like others.

Going out in crowded places, partying like others, socializing and mixing with groups, and several other things like these are standard norms. In youngsters, it is even the expected behavior. But empaths will never find it comfortable to do these due to an excessive drain on their energy levels. Thus begins the process of alienation.

Living a lonely life is not a pleasant experience for most people in this world. It is incredibly unpleasant when you are living among others and yet have no one to call as a real companion.

Most empaths struggle with this problem as expecting others to understand what they are feeling doesn't work very well.

The feeling of loneliness and longing to feel loved can take a toll on the energy levels of an empath. The empath may begin to feel even more reserved and sad.

Empath healing can help an empath recover and open up to the world. When an empath is full of positivity and energy, it becomes even more helpful in finding love and making suitable adjustments.

A Feeling of Extreme Exhaustion

There are several occasions in the life of every empath when there is no energy to venture out. You only want to stay hidden in your cove and prevent any exposure. It happens with every empath.

You may have slept well and may not have moved a muscle for some time, yet you'd feel like every muscle in your body is in pain. It will happen several times in your lifetime.

The physical exhaustion of this kind that empaths feel isn't physical at all. It is their soul aching for some energy and replenishment.

Empaths are continuously absorbing energies, feelings, and emotions of people around them. Absorbing negative vibes and emotions of people present in the vicinity has a profound impact on the energy levels of the empaths and also their souls. They may need some respite to allow their souls to recover from the strain.

Empath healing is beneficial in helping empaths recover from the exhaustion. Some empath may feel like they are only exhausted, and the things may heal on their own. However, that's living in a utopian dream. With enough rest and alone time, some energy replenishment will take place, but they may not be able to feel enthusiastic and energetic as before. They'll keep feeling exhausted very too often and may need breaks longer than before.

They must understand that it isn't their body but the soul that needs rest and healing. The sooner they begin to work on healing themselves on the energy level, the faster they'll be able to feel more productive and energized.

Filled with Negativity and Unproductive Emotions

Besides the fact that empaths have a lot of positive healing energy, they are also human beings with raw emotions of jealousy, hate, anger, resentment, etc.

It isn't uncommon for empaths to begin feeling jealous, contemptuous, angry, stressed, and anxious. These are the raw emotions that we all have. Empaths have a massive reservoir of positive energy, and hence they can keep these emotions under the surface.

However, if the empath is already low on energy or feeling exhausted and drained, it is not uncommon for these negative sentiments to take over empaths.

Empaths may also exhibit emotions like jealousy when they feel exploited and see others enjoying life at their expense. Watching others thrive in the abusive as well as highly competitive cut-throat competition can even fill them with contempt.

Empaths must try to stay away from such environments because such settings can have a toll on their personality and energy levels.

Empath Healing Is Simple

Empath healing is not a very complicated science to understand or doesn't even require elaborate preparation and setting. There are scientific and straightforward ways to allow your inner energies to heal that come under empath healing.

Losing focus and feeling ungrounded and unsettled are common malice from which most empaths struggle most of their lives. Even the empaths practicing empath healing are not immune to these. Empaths tend to feel overstimulated even from minor incidents. Situations that most people may easily ignore may have a profound impact on the hearts and minds of empaths. Various grounding techniques in empath healing can help empaths feel grounded and centered. They'd be able to exercise better control over their thoughts and emotions. Proper rest and sleep can only be possible in this state.

Keeping the mind centered is another challenge for most empaths. Their thoughts are usually a whirlpool, and there is a continuous churning. It may pose a problem for empaths as they are not able to keep their mind focused on matters of great importance and remain engaged with minor issues. Empath healing techniques like practicing mindfulness in life can help them in gaining better focus and perspective. They'll be able to look at life with a more refined lense that's not easily clouded by the repetitive thoughts of the past or their references. They can look at things from new reference points.

The biggest challenge with empaths is to unload the weight they carry on their chests and mind. The negative feelings, emotions, pain, and suffering that they absorb has consequences on their mental and emotional health. Not being able to get over these very often can lead to depression and anxiety. It is also the most significant cause of exhaustion and restlessness in empaths. Empath healing can help you process all the negative vibes, feelings, and emotions with ease. You'll be able to become efficient in this processing, and hence your downtime would be shorter, and you'll be able to venture out and mix with people with fewer inhibitions.

This book will help you understand the aspects of Empath healing that are easy to follow and effective. Most empaths are usually running after the best and most effective way to heal but are unable to practice them with any distinction and fall prey to energy lapses.

This book will help you understand and follow the actionable steps that you can follow with greater ease.

CHAPTER 2
What Does It Mean To Be An Empath?

For ordinary people and surprisingly enough even to most empaths, being an empath is an enigma.

When you try to look at empath as an empowered being, you seem to ignore the struggles an empath has to face every waking moment of their lives, and even when they are asleep. Therefore, forming an outlook that empaths are empowered beings and have it all happening their way in life is an obstructed view.

If you are an empath yourself and your personal experience of life as an empath has been full of struggles, and you fail to acknowledge any power or greatness, even you have a myopic vision. Your mind is so focused on your problems and struggles that you are unable to see the big picture and the role you can play in the scheme of things.

Although it is valid for almost anyone, there can be nothing closer to the truth that being an empath is a shade of grey and nothing white or black. An empath is a highly sensitive individual with a personality resembling a sponge. An empath cannot help but absorb pain, sufferings, feelings, and emotions of people around and feel them within. An empath shares the joy and sorrows of the world without active participation in any.

Empaths are highly sensitive people that do not even have filters placed on them. They will feel what others are feeling and experience them at the same intensity levels. This the most significant reason why being an empath can be a constant struggle. Empaths have to feel emotions like sorrow, pain, grief, and contempt without having any backing of experience.

They can quickly begin feeling overstimulated, and that can drain them of all their energy, enthusiasm, vigor, and vitality very fast.

Overexposure to Emotions

As you already know, empaths are highly sensitive people with a tendency to absorb the feelings and emotions of others. Consider the story of Midas Touch. All he ever wanted was gold. There couldn't have been a more significant boon than to be able to turn anything into gold. One day he got the boon, but there was a rider or a condition. The boon was good for everything he touched, and there were going to be no exceptions. Midas could neither have anything to eat or drink nor hug or hold anyone he loved.

He touched his beloved daughter out of love, and she turned to gold. The same happened with his food and drink. Was that anymore a boon for him?

Similar is the case of empaths. It is incredible if you can know and feel what others feel. This world is full of deceptive people. People usually try to present them differently than they are. Having the power to know their feelings and emotions can work wonders.

However, this is just one side of the story. As an empath, you can never be selective. You act as an emotional sponge. If you are in a room with five people in severe pain, you will feel the intensity of pain they are experiencing. It means that while you may be able to get helpful insights from your intuitive power, you will also experience pain that will have nothing to do with you.

It can be overwhelming for anyone. Imagine feeling sorrow, pain, grief, resentment, and other such emotions while you have no reason to be sad. These emotions don't only come as a reactionary feeling generated in empathy. Most are not even able to differentiate whether the emotion they are feeling is theirs of someone else's.

Being an empath means being a sandbox of emotions. You may be in a perfect setting to propose to your girlfriend when you get hit with intense feelings of grief. It is a possibility that you can never rule out or at least variations of it.

Therefore, besides the fact what you may have heard about empaths, this is a part that most empaths are never able to handle correctly. As a result, they face severe anxiety issues, restlessness, and even depression.

Understanding the correct ways to reinforce your energy fields, keeping yourself grounded, the proper distinction between your feelings and the feelings of others, and various other empath healing techniques can help you in dealing with this issue to a great extent.

Fear of Crowded Places

Stage fright and fear of public speaking is a common issue that many people face. Some are introverts, and they fear mixing with crowds as it is against their nature of keeping to themselves. Some people suffer from various anxiety disorders, notably social anxiety disorder, in which the victims are fearful of meeting with people.

However, the common problem they have is that they fear mixing or interacting with too many people as that can force them to come out of their comfort zones.

An empath, on the other hand, necessarily may not be an introvert. An empath may be an extrovert and steal fear crowds. It may sound contradictory, but it isn't. An empath doesn't fear interaction but the emotional overload.

Empaths are highly sensitive beings, and they usually absorb the emotions of people around them. Going in a crowd exposes them to the feelings of people present. A high number of people may mean a greater variety of emotions that may get picked. It is a reason empaths prevent going to crowded places.

It makes things challenging for empaths. Being an empath doesn't mean you can survive by living under a rock. Going out in public to get an education, earn money, and fulfill your social duty is a responsibility. It increases the risk of exposure to crowds several fold, and hence the emotional overload will increase automatically.

As an empath, besides other things, you also need to learn to cope with such situations. You have no option than to learn to differentiate between your emotions as well as the emotions you pick from others.

Even that can't guarantee prevention from exhaustion. Empath healing techniques help you learn ways to overcome this effect quickly and effectively.

Difficulty in Forming Strong Relationships

Relationships are an exchange. Stronger relationships have a fair transaction of emotions and feelings. You give love and attention, and you get the same from your partner.

It is all fine and dandy when it comes to ordinary people as they can carry out such transactions with greater efficiency. However, when it comes to empaths, things are not as simple as they might seem.

An empath is a reservoir of love and affection. Everyone that comes in contact with an empath gets some from that reservoir and gives some from theirs. However, this transaction is usually overloading the empath and depleting the energy levels. When the empath is with the partner, there may not be the energy and enthusiasm that the partner may need, and this can lead to discontent and trust issues.

Empaths need a lot of love and affection in their relationships as that helps them recharge and heal. But, it is a fact that they fear intimacy. They need a lot of breathing space in the relationships as alone time helps them heal and get over the emotional overload.

Many empaths are never able to explain this to their partners and keep feeling crushed in relationships, and it also leads to discontent and even contempt.

Having a stable and fulfilling relationship can make the life of an empath much more comfortable, but usually doesn't materialize for most empaths. Lack of communication and trust are the usual villains.

Lack of love and stable relationships thus becomes a regular feature in the lives of empaths.

Being an empath means several things that you may not come across regularly. The world primarily focuses on the positive aspects and the abilities of empaths. It doesn't care about the challenges an empath feels. However, as an empath, you also have to live with all the shortcomings too. They come as a package deal.

Being an Empath Doesn't Mean a Life of Misery

But, does that mean all empaths necessarily need to live miserable lives? Is there no way possible for an empath to lead a healthy and stable life as a person?

These are typical concerns that empaths have. Being an empath is not a curse. On the contrary, you have considerable responsibilities and powers to carry them out.

On the personal front, the struggles are entirely yours, and you will have to find ways to deal with them.

A proper distinction of emotions, firm boundaries, better communication, and routine healing are some of the ways that can help any empath a healthy life.

However, this may not be equally easy for all empaths. The reason is simple. All empaths are not the same.

Awakened empaths have acknowledgment and realization of the condition and faith in their powers. They understand the reality of being an empath and continually work on improving their lives.

Unawakened empaths, on the other hand, remain oblivious to their powers and live and die in the confusion of the things happening with them. They will have a hard time gaining control of their lives.

Usually, all empaths begin as unawakened empaths and realize their gift later on. The higher you keep moving on the empath scale, the easier it would become for you to deal with such issues. The reason is simple; the higher you move up, you get better equipped to accept the situation and begin making changes accordingly.

You must understand where you stand and then begin improving from there. The next chapter would help you understand the evolutionary journey of an empath, and you will be able to determine your position better.

CHAPTER 3
The Evolutionary Journey Of An Empath

Like everything else in this, even the road to empowerment for empath also goes through struggles. Being born as an empath doesn't open the doors of greatness. On the contrary, being born an empath and not realizing your abilities can be a significant problem. Only when you realize your potential and begin working on it that you become capable of benefiting from those abilities.

Understanding various stages of development in the life of an empath will help you understand your position and possibly the cause of your confusion at that stage.

Broadly, there are seven stages in the development of an empath's life:

Realization

It is the primary stage where you begin to realize that there is something different. Here, you do not feel joyous about being different. You know for sure that you do not feel the same as others. While people in your class, friend circle, or family may be able to mix with others, go anywhere unchecked, you don't feel comfortable in doing so. You feel constrained. You begin to feel the energy drain in going out or meeting a lot of people. Most people try to fight out their condition. They try to increase their exposure believing that facing the problem might help them overcome it. Soon most empaths realize that there is something different at which they are not able to point their fingers.

Even at this stage, very few people can realize that they are an empath. In most cases, this can happen in the early stages of development like in teens, and most people are usually confused then, and that's why people easily misunderstand it as a coming of age problem.

It is the stage of realization that you aren't like others. You may be able to pinpoint that you have problems in specific areas, but still, there is no real understanding of the situation.

Symptomatic Management

It is the second stage of development. Most empaths come to terms with the fact that there are certain things they are not comfortable handling. They understand that they need to avoid going to crowded places, mixing with others, or visiting sites with high emotional weightage like emergency rooms or hospital waiting rooms, for instance.

Empaths begin avoiding such places consciously, to make themselves more efficient or to avoid feeling overwhelmed. Even at this stage, they are not looking at the root cause of the problem but undertaking symptomatic management of the issue.

However, by this time, some empaths become more curious about their state and begin exploring more. They might also encounter terms like social anxiety disorders, highly sensitive people, and empaths. Their realm of understanding begins to expand after this. They tend to stop looking at their state as a problem, unlike the primary stage of realization.

Coming to Terms With Reality

It is the stage in which you begin to relate with signs and traits of empaths. It is the slowest and the most challenging state. There is so much useless and exaggerated information about empaths out there that an empath may take very long to pinpoint the issue precisely. For many, this process can take years.

It isn't easy to accept the fact that an ordinary life may not be possible for you. Some may even find it harsh that they'd have to bear an unwanted responsibility of healing others.

The only reassuring thing empaths discover at this stage is the presence of ways to numb the symptoms. They usually learn about various gems, stones, crystals that can help them in restoring their energy balance. From reiki and aromatherapy to different other healing techniques, this is the stage of discovery.

Once you clearly understand that you are an empath, the next step is not difficult. At this stage, it takes the longest to come out of the denial mode. Most empaths show resistance in accepting the fact that they have strengths and limitations different from ordinary people.

The Inward Focus

In this fourth stage, empaths begin the transition from being an unawakened empath to wakefulness. Empaths discover the importance of empath healing and how it can help in recovering from the wounds of the past.

It is the real state of realization. You acknowledge and accept your gift and begin working on it.

Till now, empaths have been running pillar to post for understanding the problem and finding the solution. At this stage, they realize that moving inwards can help them find the peace and stability they have been looking for all around.

They also realize that the things they have been running from are also their assets. They understand how they can enhance and use those gifts. As I said, this is the stage of realization of potential and winning over the shortcomings. Some empaths focus on learning to control these gifts and the ways to manage them better. Others get more interested in the powers and fail at proper management.

Empaths must utilize this stage for understanding that they can have complete control over their body and mind. They must realize that managing external energies is not an arduous task as they always presumed it to be.

For most empaths, this can be a very long stage. The inner journey is long, especially if you are very sensitive and fragile. Developing a complete understanding of your limitations and skills can take very long. The skills you have also need sharpening.

However, most empaths do not dislike being an empath at this stage. They discover their new self and embrace it gleefully.

Exploring Beyond the Surface

The fifth stage is also an extension of the first. In this stage, you begin to look beyond yourself. You become curious about the purpose of the whole purpose of the exercise and your role in it.

It is the stage of broadening your consciousness. Empaths begin to move toward selflessness in this stage. They start to realize that their woes aren't the biggest and their tolerance increases.

They begin embracing their gift, and the constant struggle with their own identity comes to an end.

However, this is not the end of development. Beyond this point, the real outward expansion of an empath would begin.

The Realized State

It is the second last step in the development of an empath. By this time, an empath learns to distinguish between feelings originating within and the ones coming from outside. Empaths conquer the problems leading to crowd fatigue. They do not feel bowed down by the emotions of others in that way. They know better to deal with energy overload and have ways to heal themselves.

They have firm boundaries and feel protected most of the time. They feel more connected to others and yet in complete command of their personal feelings.

It is the stage of complete control. An empath can lead a fulfilling life at this stage without any barrier. Empaths may not struggle with relationships, public appearances, or their professional lives in general.

Empaths have an outstanding balance and control at this stage. They'd also become more stable and centered.

The Shining Light

It is the stage of complete liberation for an empath. Empaths completely accept their gift at this stage, and there is no conflict. They are also in a position to use it to help themselves as well as others.

Empaths may begin reaching out to others in need of their help without the inhibitions they've had in the past. In this stage, they need not fear. They learn to manage energy levels.

They fully understand the fact that energy dips are a part of life. They know the ways to heal themselves and also have quick ways to release stress and energy pile up.

They become more productive and begin helping others without fear or apprehensions.

Every empath can reach this stage, but the way is not going to be short. There is no way to frog-jump your way to the final step.

CHAPTER 4
Being An Empath Can Be A Roller Coaster Ride

Being an empath is nothing short of a roller coaster ride. Although most people may like to believe that all empaths have similar struggles, that's not true.

As we just saw, the empaths in the first three stages have to face a lot of challenges because they have not fully come to terms with their personalities and abilities. They are only aware of the challenges, and therefore, for them, being an empath is nothing more than a challenge.

Until then, you cannot expect them to appreciate the fact that they are an empath. However, from the fourth stage onwards, there is a steady realization of the condition, and a way opens to explore the possibilities hidden behind these challenges.

Being an empath means much more than just being an individual with high sensitivities and intuition. An empath is also a human being with feelings and emotions.

An empath can get swept away by grief in even a delightful setting where everyone else is enjoying. An empath may have to bear the burden of sorrow and suffering of a lot of people. Until an empath gains complete control over his/her faculties and learns to distinguish between personal feelings and the feelings absorbed from others, life is usually challenging.

Exhaustion can become a regular feature in the lives of empaths. Not only this, but many empaths may not even be able to recognize the cause of this exhaustion and may keep focusing on incorrect issues.

While an empath may be feeling exhausted, lifeless, and lazy, there may not be any physical exertion. Empaths keep on absorbing all sorts of emotions from people around them that lead to emotional overload. It is their soul crying for help and relief and not their body.

It can happen almost instantly, and the empaths may not even get to know what hit them. Such a sudden transformation from an average lively person in a general setting to a person who will not have any more of it, the transition can be sudden and dramatic for empaths.

Such things make the lives of empaths nothing short of a roller coaster ride.

Ordinary people find it challenging to deal with their struggles. Whereas, an empath also has to walk in the shoes of others. An empath will mimic the emotions of the person he/she comes across. It is how empaths can detect if someone is in pain or trouble. But, to do so, an empath also has to share a part of that emotion.

An empath can get physically ill in crowds. Has it ever happened that you got similar symptoms of the disease as someone very sick near you?

Do you get emotional hangovers after fights and arguments?

Are you capable of feeling what others might be feeling without them telling you about it?

Do you find it hard to differentiate between your emotions and the emotions of others?

Do you experience severe mood swings very often?

All these are signs that you need much more than mere symptomatic relief. Such signals would keep appearing, and you'd need to address them individually until you begin working on overall improvement.

CHAPTER 5
Empaths And Emotions- Things To Heal Emotional Triggers

Empaths and emotions go hand in hand. Empaths are highly sensitive, and hence emotions always play a significant role in their lives. However, there's a difference.

While ordinary people are better at passing on emotions, the empaths do not show that skill. Emotions tend to stick on them and have an overwhelming effect,

Empaths may feel tremendous pressure of carrying the emotions that may not even belong to them, but they have a hard time differentiating. It means that they can be on the brink of explosion most of the time as this is a usual affair for them.

Most empaths begin to think that they've had enough of it. Empaths even become highly sensitive to emotional triggers as even minute things start to infuriate them.

What most people fail to understand is that living as an empath, especially an unawakened empath isn't easy. Empaths are continuously dealing with issues from early childhood, and there comes a time when the empaths begin to think that they've had enough, and they become reserved and close themselves from the outer world. It doesn't do any good to anyone else and turns out to be very bad for the empath in question.

Loneliness and Alienation in Empaths

Loneliness and alienation in empaths is a common phenomenon. Although this is contradictory to their role in society, yet they feel they have no choice.

Most empaths remain closed and do not like to mix with others. Most people want to believe that it just happens because they tend to absorb the emotions of others. That's not a correct fact in its entirety. Mixing in crowds or coming in contact with too many people makes them feel exhausted and emotionally overwhelmed. Still, it is not the only reason to make empaths feel lonely and excluded. It also happens when the empaths begin to think that they don't fit in or do not belong.

It is a must that an empath has a clear understanding of the reasons that can force him/her to become a loner or begin to feel excluded and alienated.

The Reasons Empaths Begin to Feel Lonely

A Tendency to Build Walls for Protection: Renowned poet Robert Frost in his famous poem 'Mending Wall,' said that when we construct walls around us, the distinction of whether we are walling things out or walling things inside gets muddled.

Feeling overwhelmed by the exposure to large gatherings and crowds is a real problem. However, when empaths begin to wall themselves in some enclosure, they tend to invite loneliness. There is no way for people to reach out to them.

Desperate Attempts to Make Themselves Look Normal by Trying to Lower Sensitivities: This is another typical attempt teenagers or young empaths try to make themselves widely acceptable. It usually doesn't work. You are a highly sensitive individual when you go out in the crowds or try to behave normally; your exposure to emotions and feelings is going to increase for sure. Empaths try to numb their sensitivities to counter the effect. It is again against their nature, and most empaths eventually feel the pain of being caught between a rock and a hard place. The result is not good as they are not able to act cool for long and then become a confirmed loner.

A Poor Distinction Between Personal Pain and Pain of Others: It is one of the most common issues. Most empaths are unable to differentiate between their pain and the pain and suffering they pick from others. If they do not learn to distinguish, they'll shy away from public exposure. Walling themselves in isn't a solution. They must learn to differentiate between the pain emanating from the self and the one coming from outside. It is the only way they'll be able to lead a social life.

Broken Empaths: It is a category of empaths not widely known to the outside world, but it is a big category. The empaths who have witnessed too much arguing, aggression, violence tend to form the impression that they're going to get the same from the rest of the world, and they become loners. Something inside them feels damaged, and such empaths need to come out of their cocoons more importantly. If such empaths remain sulking all by themselves for too long, they may turn toward addictions.

Unpredictable and Unsafe Childhood: Childhood is a highly sensitive period. Kids, in general, are highly impressionable and empath more so. If they have an unguided and unprotected childhood with too many people around them, they might begin to form that as a general idea of people. It can make them think that staying alone is much better.

Allowing the Past to Prevail Over the Present: The past is never going to come back again. All we need to do is take lessons from the past. However, some empaths with unguided childhood, memories of exploitation, and violence tend to store that past in their minds. It acts as a part of the survival mechanism. They tend to avoid anything that resembles those memories, and you can be sure that it means practically everything.

These are just some of the reasons empaths begin to feel unsafe and unprotected. The protective mechanism comes in the form of loneliness.

However, the most significant impact it has is on the emotional stability of the empaths. They become more emotionally vulnerable.

Locking yourself under seven locks can't be a guarantee to safety. You are not only locking yourself everything out, but you are also locking yourself in a perimeter.

Empaths need to understand that they need not fear everything in this world. They only need to understand the emotional triggers that make them feel emotionally insecure and unstable. If they are getting too many emotional triggers, it can affect their emotional-health and further actions as well.

Empaths need to learn the ways to deal with such triggers and overcome the limitations they feel.

Some actionable and straightforward steps can help you as an empath to deal with the emotional triggers that you come across in your everyday lives.

Ways to Deal With Emotional Triggers

Stop Overthinking: Humankind, in general, has developed this survival mechanism where it can think and overthink anything to such an extent that the result would always be negative. It was a mechanism to help see if there were any real dangers in the future. However, we tend to overuse this future even today when we are living in a relatively safer and secure world. Empaths take this one step further and always begin to draw wrong conclusions as they are already insecure about many things due to high sensitivities.

When empaths come across a problem, they tend to become overly engaged with that problem in a negative sense. Empaths are thinking and living it within their minds. The result is always going to be dissatisfactory because our minds will always project that problem as more prominent than you. It is how our mind works. It wants to protect you, and hence demotivating you from engaging is the easy way out. It can also fill you with fear, dread, incompetence, inadequacy, and other such negative feelings. It's not a good way to deal with the problem.

An empath must not overthink a problem. If there are negative thoughts about anything, try to divert your mind elsewhere. Even a little diversion from that topic will help you look at that problem with a fresh perspective. It would be best if you did not get hooked on to a single.

On the contrary, try to think about positive things. Trying to solve the problem is always going to be more productive than excessively pondering about the issue.

Be Positive: It is easier said than done, and an empath doesn't have an option. There will be terrible and dreadful things in the world, and everyone can brood over them. However, that is not going to solve anything. The ray of hope is in looking at the positive outcomes and moving forward. As an empath, you must remain focused on finding the positives of any action. Try to draw positive lessons from every incident that you witness, and emotional stability will become a reality for you.

It would help if you remembered that for an empath to function, there will be a need for high emotional stability. You can't have that while your mind remains fixated on the negatives. The more positivity you try to propagate outside, the same would reflect within you. Therefore, you must neither remain focused on the negatives, not even keep discussing it with others. Even if they are thinking poorly about things, that would also get reflected in your heart.

Therefore, thinking about the positive aspects of even the poorest of events is a great way to condition your mind to be capable of dealing with negative things.

Become Aware: There are moments when we begin relying on what others are saying and stop paying attention to our own beliefs. Very often, it happens when we get criticized. Although we don't want to believe anything told to us, our mind starts playing that on a loop. Empaths are always looking for public validation in their early stages, and criticism is just the opposite.

It can break an empath and pave the way for seclusion. However, that is not the way an empath must behave. If someone has criticized you, look inwards and try to find if that's a reality. Most criticisms do not have immediate actions as a ground. Looking towards the cause within and not seeking validation from outside is a better way to prevent loneliness.

Forgive and Move On: Holding grudges is not for empaths. If there is something that has caused hurt, it is always better to forgive it and move on. Do not hold it for too long in your heart as that can make you contemptuous. Even if you felt terrible, keeping it into your heart would fill you with negative energy. In your heart, it can drain you. You'll begin feeling overwhelmed all too often and may also not want to venture out and help others. Holding grudges is against the nature of empaths.

Learn to Surrender and Disengage: There will be things in life that won't allow you a victory and keep you occupied. Most conflicts with your loved ones and from your bad habits are like this. They don't let you win and also keep using up your energy. You remain occupied with them for unreasonably long periods. They are a significant energy drain and also curtailing your development. It will be better if you can learn to surrender to such things and disengage. Such conflicts never have a result, and there is no way you can be victorious. The sooner you disengage, the faster you'll be able to feel free again, and that would also take away a lot of load from your chest. An empath already has too much emotional burden, and asking for more is never prudent.

Smiling is Infectious: Emoaths must learn the power of smiling too often. Most empaths are always feeling overburdened by the weight of the world. They can feel the gloom of the world in their heart but do not understand that transfer of energy works both ways. If they can feel the sorrow of the world and become sad, even the world can smile with them. You must smile too often if you want to feel positive. Most people think that smiling in stressful conditions is challenging. Indeed it is. But, you must also understand that when you smile, you radiate that positive energy to the people around you, and it is collectively going to come back to you. You can make even the most stressful situations light.

Try Methods to Keep Your Mind and Heart Calm: There are several ways to keep your mind fixed to the present and take your focus away from the past. You can try mindfulness and meditation. These methods help take away all your stress and make you feel positive and grounded.

If there are instances where you feel highly agitated or disturbed, or you feel that negativity is taking over you, rhythmic breathing and 'pranayama' are excellent ways to get over such feelings.

Deep breathing is at the core of meditation practices. Breathing is vital for life. In the thick and thin of our lives, we tend to forget the importance of this crucial process. We begin feeling that other things are so important. But we are wrong.

You can survive without the people you love for very long. Most people think they won't or can't, but the reality is that they can. You can even survive without food for days or even months. There are instances where people have survived for more than two months on complete fast. You can even survive without a drop of water for three days. However, you can't survive without breathing air, even for a few minutes. When you can't breathe, you realize that it is the most crucial process to live.

Breathing not only provides oxygen to the body, but it also helps you calm down. It is the reason breathing plays such a crucial role in all meditation practices. It enables you to calm the mind and bring the focus at one point.

When we feel agitated, excited, angry, or overstimulated, the first thing to go out of control is your breathing. Your breathing becomes rapid and erratic. At that point, your body is trying to cope up with this overstimulation.

Through deep breathing, we will try to make breathing calm. When you breathe rhythmically, the mind gets a better chance to cope up with the trouble at hand, and it has less to handle. Rhythmic breathing can help you in resolving anger, anxiety, and stress.

Though the process of deep and rhythmic breathing, we will focus on lowering the mounting pressure on the system. It will increase the supply of oxygen in your body and also reduce the blood pressure that begins to rise in such situations.

Relaxed Rhythmic Breathing

Rhythmic breathing is a simple exercise. You do not need any skill for that. We know how to breathe since we came to the world. In moments of excitement, we lose our focus on our breathing and begin to pay attention to other elements. Rhythmic breathing helps in calming the mind and prevents emotions prevailing over your senses.

- Whenever you begin to feel overstimulated or sense emotions taking over you
- Bring your awareness to the process of breathing
- Do not try to think anything
- Only focus on your breath
- It is like counting your breaths
- You only need to observe your breathing
- Do not try to control your breathing
- Three is no need to force your breath
- Become aware of your breathing
- Observe whether you are breathing rapidly
- It is alright even if you are breathing fast
- Just focus your awareness on your breath
- Watch the air coming in
- And, then observe it going out
- Try to feel your breath
- Sense the warmth it has
- Try to take notice if there is anything different
- While you do this
- You might have some thoughts and emotions
- Do not try to force those thoughts and emotions
- Do not engage with them
- Even trying to take your mind off those thoughts is engagement
- You do not need to engage with them
- Only focus on your breathing
- Just acknowledge the thoughts in your mind
- And, bring your awareness back to your breathing
- Breathe in and breathe out
- Repeat it as many times as you may like
- The more you focus on your breathing
- The calmer you'll get

- Your engagement with your thoughts would go down
- As you breathe with greater focus, your breathing would become more in-depth and slower
- Don't try to change anything or force your breathing pattern
- Try to find your natural breathing pace
- Remain focused on your breath until your breathing returns to normal
- You can take your time
- There is no rush
- It is your body and your breathing
- No one is a witness to it
- It is also the best way to go into the meditative state
- Through this method, your mind will become focused, and you will have better control over your thoughts and emotions

It is a simple breathing exercise, and you can do it anytime you want. Doing it when you are feeling agitated, excited, angry, or emotional is highly effective. It prevents you from getting obsessed with the problem. The more focused you get on the situation at hand, the less likely you are to find a solution. Continuously thinking about it will make it larger than it is in reality.

This rhythmic breathing exercise will help you divert your attention from the problem, and once the immediate phase passes over, you will be able to look at the problem with a broader perspective.

Rhythmic breathing also helps in calming the mind chatter. You'll feel at peace. It is also a great exercise to relax your mind and relieve stress. This exercise can be beneficial in coping with stressful situations.

Pranayama

Breathing exercises in Yoga can also play a fantastic role in calming the mind, increasing focus, and building command over your abilities. Breathing exercises in Pranayama, like breathing through alternate nostrils, victorious breathing, female honey bee humming breath, and bellows breath, can help you focus entirely on your breath.

Although you'll need to form a routine to perform these exercises in the morning, they can have several benefits, like:
- Lower stress
- Improved Mindfulness
- Better sleep quality
- Better Brain Function
- Control in High Blood Pressure

- Improved Lung Function

Each exercise in Pranayama has its specific advantages. For instance, female honey bee humming breath can help in managing high blood pressure efficiently. Victorious breath exercise can help you in building a better focus, achieving a meditative state, energizing the body and the mind, and having significant control over your senses.

Out of these four, the most important for you can be alternate nostril breathing. It is a fantastic breathing exercise for reducing stress and anxiety. This exercise alone can help you in dealing with energy imbalance in the body as well as bring mental clarity. It also helps in calming the body and the mind. You'll feel rejuvenated, and offloading emotions would become more manageable.

- The best time to practice alternate nostril breathing is in the morning and evening
- However, it is a very calming practice, but if you are feeling highly agitated or overstimulated, you can practice it at any time of the day at any place where you can find peace.
- Practicing alternate nostril breathing very easily
- Please sit in a cross-legged posture
- If you are unable to take a full-lotus position, you can also sit with your legs crossed comfortably
- Before you begin alternate nostril breathing, it is essential to calm your breathing
- Once you have a natural breathing rhythm
- Hold your nostril from one hand
- It will be easier if you choose your active hand for the same
- You can place your other hand in your lap in a resting position
- Ensure your back and neck are straight
- To practice alternate nostril breathing, fold your index finger and middle finger and make their tips touch the palm at the base of your thumb
- You can use the thumb to press the nostril at its side
- You can use the ring finger and the little finger of that hand to press the nostril of the other side
- Now place your thumb on one of the nostrils and close it
- From the other nostril inhale deeply
- Release the nostril covered by your thumb
- Now using your middle finger close the other nostril and exhale fully

- From this nostril itself, inhale deeply
- Cover this nostril now and use the other nostril to exhale and inhale
- You will need to repeat this process several times

Alternate nostril breathing is effortless to perform, and it can play a vital role in calming your mind and ensuring the proper flow of energy and oxygen in the body.

Controlled Breathing

If you are feeling very anxious at any time of the day or getting overwhelmed by emotions, you can also practice controlled breathing. It is an easy way to get over anxieties. It will help you calm down instantly and even override strong emotions. You do not need any special preparation for controlled breathing. Even if you are feeling anxious in bed and unable to sleep due to fearful or overpowering thoughts, controlled breathing can be of great help.

- You can sit in a relaxed position or even lie down on the bed
- The purpose of controlled breathing is to take your mind away from engaging thoughts
- The thoughts are either good or bad they can prevent thoughts
- Controlled breathing can help you calm down and have a relaxed sleep
- Begin by inhaling deep
- Please do not do it fast
- Inhale as slowly as possible
- Fill in as much air as you can
- While you are inhaling, you must remain mindful of the movement of the air through your nostrils
- Imagine the air you are breathing as a ray of light
- With your awareness, follow the path it takes in your body
- Feel it filling your lungs
- See how it makes your chest expand as more and more ail fills in it
- Do not stop until there is any space left to fill in more air
- Now hold your breath for a brief moment
- Once you are full
- Do not release the air immediately
- Count in your mind till 5

- 1....2....3.....4.....5
- You might feel the pressure building inside you
- This pressure is good
- Just hold it a little longer
- Once you feel that you can't hold it any longer
- Start to release air through your mouth very slowly
- You must try to push out all the air inside you
- Empty all the air in your gut
- Feel your chest getting deflated
- Repeat the process several times
- The exhalations will help you feel light
- They will take away all the stress, anxiety, and overpowering thoughts
- The exhalations would make you feel lighter

This breathing process is beneficial in calming the mind. You might be having some very overpowering thoughts at that moment. You do not need to worry about them. While you are following controlled breathing, you may get distracting thoughts. It is normal to have them. You do not need to fight such thoughts. Acknowledge those thoughts but ignore them.

When you are inhaling air to the brim and holding it for a while, all such thoughts will pass. Nothing is more important than breathing. Those thoughts will have no power over you. As you exhale, all the stress would go out. You'll find calm prevailing over you.

These are simple breathing exercises that can help you a lot in building deep focus, and they also help in achieving the meditate state faster.

Meditation to Heal Your Heart Chakra and to keep Your Emotions calm

Meditation To Heal the Heart Chakra

Please sit in a cross-legged posture
Place your hands in your lap
Keep the palms facing upwards
You can also keep your hands on your knees
Please sit in an upright position
Try to keep your spine during the whole meditation session
If you wish, you can use a backrest
Please do not use a backrest
Please keep your neck straight
Your shoulders should be aligned, but that shouldn't cause stress
Now gently close your eyes
Do not put pressure on your eyes

Keep them closed gently
Gather all your thoughts
Collect them in your mind
Then allow them to go away
Do not hold your thoughts
You do not need them for now
Take your time
There is no hurry
There can be thoughts, allow them to pass
It is not the time for thoughts
It is time for awareness
Focus your awareness to your breath
Take a deep and gentle breath in
Slowly leave it out
It is a beautiful process of life
You do not need to think about anything else
No worries mean anything
Embrace breathing with awareness
It is the most beautiful and essential process of life
We will practice deep breathing
Breathe gently
Breathe deeply through your nose, slowly and gently
Breathe in
Allow it to travel through your nose to your gut
Hold it there for a brief moment
Then, very slowly and steadily
Breathe out through your mouth
Do not rush the process
Be gentle
Breathe in
Breathe out
All this while
Let your awareness follow your breathing
Follow the air goes in and comes out
Feel the air
Its warmth
The fragrance it has
The sound it makes while entering your nostrils
There is nothing more important than this air
It is the life-force
The energizer
Feel the air coming in and the calm it brings
Breathe in
Breathe out
Keep your awareness glued to your breath

No thought is essential at this point
Just immerse yourself in the process
Breathe in
Breathe out
Follow the path of this air in your body
See the light that enters with the air
Follow that light
Feel the way it fills your lungs
Sense the way it inflates your chest
Look at the way it fills up your stomach
Now hold it for a few moments
Let this air revitalize your body
Let it rejuvenate your body
Sense the calm around you
There is no rush
There is no hurry
Relax completely
When you breathe out, feel all the negative energy going out with the breath
Cherish the relaxation of the spent air going out
Take a deep breath again
Very slowly and gradually
Imagine the soothing fresh air filling your body
Let it light up your whole body
This light will illuminate you from inside and remove all the negativity
Follow this light that's traveling inside your body along with the air
Follow its path
Watch it fill your stomach
Witness how it has illuminated your spine and your back
Observe it flowing through your body
Feel every nerve and muscle in your body through your awareness
Hold your breath for a few moments
Do not release it quickly
Let the fresh air seep in
Now, exhale very slowly
Feel every negative thought going out with the breath
This air will take away all the negative energy and restore the balance
It will repair every damage that has happened
Feel the calm inside you
Enjoy this calm and relaxation for a few moments we will begin when you are ready
Now focus on your heart chakra
The heart is the center of emotions
It pumps blood in the whole body
It also makes you feel every emotion

It can get heavy
It can get overwhelmed
It is time to make it feel light
It is time to relieve some pressure from your heart
It is time you released some load off your chest
Green color represents the heart chakra
Green is the color of prosperity
It is the color that fills the world with happiness
It is the color of nature
It is the color of the soothing energy
When you peer deep
You'll also see pink
Appreciate the beauty of this contrast
It is the nature of love
So much love coming out from such a small dot
Love is overpowering
But it is also forgiving
It is all-absorbing
Focus your attention again on the spread of the green color
It has covered you completely
You are now full of love
All covered in it
All drenched in love
No place left dry
There will be no desperation
You won't need anyone else to feel loved
You have the ocean of love inside you
You are the reservoir that can fill this world with love
Feel the comfort it is providing to your heart
There is no room for contempt now
There is no need for grudges
You don't need to ask love from anyone
You have all the love you need in this world
Look how beautiful things have become after getting drenched in this green color
This green color is healing every wound
It is providing the comfort you needed
Now you know you can get it whenever you want
Let it spread to every corner of your body
Let it spread even out of your body
You have it in limitless quantity
It wouldn't come to an end
Forgive anyone who didn't give it back
Share it with anyone who needs it
Feel the love inside you

You are feeling calm now
It is a relaxing feeling
This calm is complete
It doesn't rely on others
You have forgiven everyone who has hurt you
You only have love and compassion for them now
As the green light evaporates, you are feeling light
You are completely relaxed now
There is no stress
There is no longing
There is no wanting
There is just calm
You are positive now
Bath in the glory of this new energy
Let it drench you
Relish the feeling and relax
Inhale slowly through your nose
Exhale even slower through your mouth
Inhale slowly through your nose
Exhale even slower through your mouth
Inhale slowly through your nose
Exhale even slower through your mouth
Let your breathing return to normal
Keep breathing slowly
Open your eyes slowly when you are ready
You can practice this meditation every day to feel calm and loved. The more pleasant and positive you feel within, the better control you'll have of yourself.

CHAPTER 6
Empaths And Addictions- The Why And How Of Getting Out Of It

For some people, empaths and addictions may go hand in hand. The presumption is not misplaced. It is a fact that a very high number of empaths give in to various kinds of addictions.

When we hear the term addiction, it is usual to think of smoking, alcohol, and drug abuse. It is a harsh reality that most empaths do indulge in these kinds of addictions. Anything that helps them numb their sensitivities for a while or make them less sensitive to energies around them is easy to pick. However, it is only one part of the story. It is crucial that you also understand the cause.

Empaths are highly sensitive. Most empaths find it challenging to cope with crowded places, too much interaction, and overwhelming emotions that they invariably pick from the people around them. It can make their social lives highly challenging. But, they have no other option to be in such circumstances. It can take a toll on their energy levels and make them feel exhausted. Most empaths live lonely lives to deal with such problems. But, a person cannot avoid such things forever. Empaths also have to be in crowded places and mix with people. It is due to this that they start to seek measures to numb their senses.

Hence, addictions seem to be an easy choice for empaths dealing with such stressful situations.

When a person turns to any method of addiction, the prime objective is to experience relief and happiness. Drugs and alcohol lower your inhibitions and sensitivities. As a result, even an empath finds it easy to mix with people and bear all the things that are very tough to handle when in a full sense. Such things lead to dopamine release in the brain that relaxes the body and mind. It has a numbing effect.

However, these are not the only things that can produce such an effect. Anything that has an immersive impact can create a similar result, and that's why you can find several other things to which an empath can get addicted.

Empaths can also find other ways to cope with their stress. Some empaths find solace in food while others get addicted to shopping. You may have your poison of choice, but the impact is the same. All these things only push you towards more profound isolation, and loneliness and the desire to cope with the challenges get buried under these addictions completely.

However, giving in to such addictions cannot be the way. The problem with these addictions is that they keep on increasing your dependency on them, and you are never able to come out of them. They harm your personality and development.

Understanding the Way Your Brain Works

Most people live in the misconception that it is the substance or relief mechanism that makes them cope up with the challenges they are trying to avoid. They forget that the challenges are always there. Any addiction that they have is only a temporary shield, and it never has an impact on the problem.

If you absorb emotions from people around you and heavy drinking seems to be a solution to that problem, then you are wrong. Drinking doesn't make you immune; it just makes you insensitive. The moment you are out of the influence of alcohol, you'll have the same problems. You might even feel more embarrassed to go in front of those people due to the things you might have done in an inebriated state.

The same is the case with people trying to find solace in food. They find it difficult to go out in public and choose food as their sulking time companion. Soon, that overdependence on food brings more problems like obesity and other health concerns, and they might feel even more concerned about going out in public.

Some people like to find a resolution of their stress and anxiety in shopping. They indulge in shopping for things they don't even need. It doesn't provide any solution to their problems, only offers a distraction to their mind from the things that are bothering them at that moment.

These addictions have no impact on your problem. They are just changing the way you look at the difficulties and numb your sensitivities for a while.

Your brain is capable of doing all that and much more even without any addiction.

Several studies suggest that all the substances and habits that we pick to cope with our challenges only stimulate our brain to release dopamine, serotonin, and other such chemicals in the brain. These are happy hormones that induce a 'feel good' sensation.

Everyone seeks happiness, peace, and liberation. Even an ordinary person is always striving to find peace and happiness. Addictions become even more desirable for empaths who are under immense emotional strain most of the time.

Empaths who are usually under great emotional pain are always aching for such ease, and that's why they feel more inclined to fall for smoking, alcohol, and drugs.

It doesn't matter whether you find relief by using banned narcotics, legal but harmful things like alcohol and smoke, interventions like painkillers, or even turn to comfort foods, none of these help you at all. The real relief comes when your mind recognizes such substances and releases dopamine.

You got that right; our minds can manufacture dopamine on their own without the help of these methods.

If you are calm, the mind keeps releasing it at a steady pace. However, stress and anxiety can inhibit the dopamine release, and you may find yourself aching for relief.

The more stressed, anxious, and emotionally drained you feel, the greater would be the need to have something to calm your senses. At the same time, your mind would completely stop the production and release of the 'feel-good' hormone.

The most important thing to note here is that it isn't the ability to be happy and calm that you lack. Your mind is capable of inducing that calm and happiness on its own, and it doesn't need any help. The only thing lacking is the correct state of mind in which it can release those hormones.

Whether You Want to Be a Push Start Engine or a Self-Start One

The choice is yours, whether you want to be a push start engine that needs an external stimulant to make you feel happy or can become a self-start engine that can work on its own.

It is ok to feel that it isn't so simple. I've been there once. It seems as if the world is going to come crashing down on the head. Most empaths feel that the worst part is managing the hypersensitivities. They are wrong.

The hypersensitivities are a boon and not a bane. The problem is not in your being hypersensitive but your abilities to manage those hypersensitivities. If you have control of your sensitivities and you are in a position to use them to help yourself as well as others, would you complain about them even then?

The root cause of the problem is poor management of the abilities. Most empaths keep feeling overwhelmed by emotions, and they are never able to recognize that there are ways to manage those emotions.

Addictions of all kinds are escape routes taken by empaths to avoid fatigue caused by overwhelming emotions. Only if they could manage these emotions would they realize that there are ways to prevent such fatigue easily.

It would help if you had the clarity of the ability to feel pleasant and joyful is always there in your mind. You don't need to get stoned or drink like a fish to feel calm. Your mind can do that on its own with great ease. You only need to keep your nerves quiet. Hence, your objective is to learn ways to keep stress and anxiety low and stay calm. You would need to understand the ways to avoid emotional overload and also the ways to release the emotions picked from the surroundings.

Addictions are destructive, but we all know that already. The need is to find a solution to the problem. Deaddiction centers and support groups can help you in leaving the addictions for the moment, but they do not address the root causes. The reason for turning toward these addictions is the inability to cope with them or to manage them. However, that doesn't imply that the ways to do so don't exist.

Empaths can deal with addictions in a better way if they begin taking the measures given below.

Steps to Avoid Emotional Overload Leading to Addictions

Relax. Take a Break Often: We all know that empaths can begin to feel overloaded with emotions very often. They act as emotional sponges, and hence the more they come in contact with others, the faster they begin to feel exhausted and drained. It is hard to avoid as an empath. Awakened empaths learn to deal with this problem as they have a better mechanism to differentiate between their emotions and emotions absorbed from others. However, most empaths may not be able to do that. But, they can take breaks more often to allow their system to handle the stress.

Do not hesitate to withdraw yourself from stressful situations so that your system doesn't begin to feel overwhelmed. It might feel awkward and embarrassing in the beginning, but it can help you a lot in working for longer in such circumstances.

Unload: An empath will have to learn ways to release the excess emotional burden as it accumulates. It may not look straightforward, but as an empath, you do not have an option. Several ways can help you in releasing the accumulated emotions. Crying, shouting it out loudly, and breathing exercises are some of the ways that can help you in removing the emotions causing negative thoughts.

You do not need to keep everything inside you. Meditation is also a fantastic way to center your brain and feel grounded.

Become Mindful: Mindfulness is the way to become more attentive to the things happening around you and pay closer attention to them. Most of us keep living in our thoughts and become obsessed with our assessments drawn from those thoughts. It is a habit that will only push us towards negative thoughts.

Becoming mindful will help you in taking everything that comes across on its face value. You stop being judgemental about things, and there remains no need to overanalyze things.

When you become mindful, you will be in a better position to evaluate your impulses and not move toward addictions so fast.

Mindfulness is not a trick but a way of life. It'll take some time for you to become fully mindful of your actions and thoughts, but you aren't an empath for a season either. You must begin practicing mindfulness in your actions and thoughts as early as possible if you want to stay away from addictions forever.

Become a Doer Rather Than a Seer: One of the most notable drawbacks of having high cognitive abilities is that people begin to rely on their mind more and reduce the focus on actions. In their minds, they begin to evaluate everything rigorously; the conclusion is mostly not to take any action at all. Their emphasis on physical activity is so little that it also leads to an imbalance of energies in their bodies.

It will help if you become physically active. Devote some time for exercise and gym regularly. You can also do Yoga and meditation. Playing outdoor games of any kind is also helpful.

If your body is also equally tired as your body due to physical work, there will be a balance in energies, and you'll find it easy to sleep and relax. Also, while you are working out or engaged in any physical work, your mind will focus more on the job at hand and less on the thoughts in your mind. It will also help you find a different perspective when you again have that thought.

Remaining engaged in anything physically would help you in preventing the urge toward addictions.

Focus on the Gift: Even the most precious thing in this would be a burden on you if you don't know its use. The same is the case with your empathic abilities. You have a gift, and you must explore that gift and enhance it.

Until you acknowledge your gift and begin utilizing it, you'll remain burdened by it. Once you learn the art of using that gift, you'll find it much easier to handle your energies. There will be no stress on your system, and you'll also be better at finding peace for yourself. Once that happens, you'll see that there is no need for depending on addictions.

Help for Food and Shopping Addicts

There is no doubt that fighting addiction is never going to be an easy fear for any empath. Coming to terms with the fact that you are different and would remain so for the rest of your life isn't easy. However, every empath must understand that there is no other way to deal with this problem. Giving in to addictions is only going to open the gates of the dark cave that doesn't have an opening of hope.

You have a gift for which others would be ready to trade anything. However, that gift comes with some burdens. The real trick is to find a balance and not in hiding under the temporary shade of addictions.

People who are struggling with addictions of other kinds, like food and shopping addictions, also face similar problems or even more complex ones.

They know that they overeat only to cope with their emotions, but they know no other way to deal with it. On the other hand, society doesn't even consider food and shopping as dangerous or self-destructive habits, and hence such people find very little motivation to get over such addictions. Every food or shopping addict empath must understand that these aren't coping mechanisms, but a way devised to keep them distracted from the problem.

Overdependence on these habits is going to take you down one day.

Overeaters must work on their diet and improve their food intake. A high intake of protein and fat-rich food and a lower intake of refined carbs and sugary items will help them in preventing food cravings. Increasing the quantity of fiber-rich food in their diet will also help.

Empaths must understand that it isn't the lack of energy that they suffer but an excess of it. They do not need to keep eating all the time to feel more energetic. They only need to learn ways to overcome emotions, and their energy levels would automatically become balanced.

The same is the case with shopping addicts. They shop to divert their mind from the emotions overpowering them. But the harder they try, the more influential the feelings would become. You would need to understand that all this is going inside your very head, and there are no secrets. Meditation and breathing exercises can help you better in dealing with these emotions rather than a spending spree that might give you another kind of headache later.

CHAPTER 7
Empaths And Stress- Battling Sleeplessness And Fatigue

Exhaustion, fatigue, irritation, body aches, anxiety, and stress are some of the issues that many empaths may face regularly. These do not look like huge problems as most of us might feel tired, exhausted, tired, and irritated at the end of the day. But, what if you begin to have all these as soon as you wake up.

Many empaths may experience these symptoms even as they wake up after a full night's sleep. These are clear signals that the empath is suffering from adrenal fatigue.

What Is Adrenal Fatigue?

The human body is a miracle. It is a highly complex machine that has a system to counter every situation. When you are in real danger, you may find superhuman strength. However, in normal conditions, the body works very efficiently, saving every drop of energy.

There are specific glands in the body to regulate stress in the body called the adrenal glands. Stress has a crucial role to play in our body. When you are under any danger or stressful situation, the adrenal glands sense this and begin releasing the stress hormone called 'cortisol' to enable you to cope with that situation.

For instance, if suddenly a wild animal comes in front of you, the only way out is to run fast. But, we all know that generally, all quadrupeds can run faster than us. However, the body acknowledges the emergency, and it begins pumping cortisol in large quantities. The hormone makes your heart pump more quickly, which means your lower limbs would get more oxygenated blood for giving your faster speed. Not only this, but the blood vessels in your body also constrict and divert most of the blood to your muscles so that they can give better energy output. Cortisol also leads to temporary insulin resistance. In this state, the cells in the body that utilize the glucose present in the bloodstream are unable to use it. All the glucose in the bloodstream becomes available to the muscles. Your blood pressure also increases, making overall blood circulation much faster.

All this happens just for the sake of making you faster. Hence, the stress in the body is not a useless effect. The adrenal gland has its essential role not only in making you more combative in stressful situations but also in general.

The timely release of stress hormones keeps you sharp, focused, and decisive. However, the adrenals can only function well if you can manage your stress properly. If you begin to suffer from chronic stress, the adrenals will have to keep producing stress hormones all the time, and they'll get overworked. This condition is called adrenal fatigue.

The Reason, Most Empaths, Suffer From Adrenal Fatigue

It is no surprise that most empaths suffer from adrenal fatigue. The reason for that is straightforward. Empaths not only carry the burden for stress in their day to day lives but also act as sponges and keep absorbing the feelings and emotions of people around them. They are highly sensitive beings, and that also makes them more susceptible to high stress. It leads to a chronic stress situation.

Because their adrenals have to keep producing more and more stress hormones like cortisol, there comes a time when they become incapable of keeping up with the demand. This condition is adrenal fatigue. An empath suffering from this condition may experience tiredness, grogginess, exhaustion, anxiety, stress, irritability, and dizziness.

Some people may also experience heart palpitations leading to severe anxiety, blood pressure fluctuations, and even delirium.

For the body to function correctly, the stress hormone levels should be high in the morning. During our sleep, the production of the cortisol hormone is at its peak, and that's why people feel sharp, fresh, and energetic in the morning. As the day passes by, the cortisol level goes down, and you begin to feel tired by the end of the day. However, this happens in ideal scenarios when the person is not facing chronic stress.

During chronic stress, the adrenals never cease to stop producing cortisol, and even in the evening, the cortisol levels are high. It can make you feel anxious, sleepless, and alert. It can cause insomnia and sleep difficulties.

Dealing with adrenal fatigue is very important as overworked adrenals may not be able to produce cortisol hormones in the required quantity. This condition is called adrenal insufficiency. It will again lead to lethargy, tiredness, and exhaustion. In such a state, your body may not be able to regulate some of the vital things like

- Burning fat and protein
- Maintaining ideal blood pressure
- Regulation of sugar
- Reacting to stressors

Lower production of stress hormones in the body is bad news as it can lead to several health disasters.

The symptoms of adrenal fatigue and insufficiency are:

- Weakness
- Brain fog
- Difficulty in sleeping
- Difficulty in waking up

- Fatigue
- Loss of appetite
- Salt and sugar cravings
- Lightheadedness
- Lack of motivation
- Unexplained weight loss
- Hair loss
- Extreme blood pressure fluctuations

Ways to Counter Adrenal Fatigue, Sleeplessness, and Stress

We have understood the problems that may arise if you suffer from adrenal fatigue. However, the critical part is to understand the solutions. Adrenal fatigue is a common problem suffered by people going through chronic stress, which is the story of most empaths who are still under struggle.

However, some measures can help you in fighting adrenal fatigue.

Dietary Changes: When the stress level is high, it can lead to insulin resistance, which is another major health issue as it can lead to prediabetes and diabetes. More than 110 million Americans currently suffer from this condition, and a very high number of them remain ignorant about it as there are no prominent symptoms. However, this condition is not harmless. It can have a devastating impact on your health. To lower insulin resistance and cortisol levels, you must make appropriate dietary changes. The following changes can be beneficial:

- Increase the consumption of whole foods
- Increase fruits and vegetables in your diet
- Focus on consuming fat and protein-rich diet

It would be best if you lowered the consumption of:
- Simple carbohydrates or refined carbs
- Processed foods
- Deep-fried food
- Caffeine

Adopting these dietary changes would help you in lowering insulin resistance, which also helps in reducing the cortisol levels, and addressing adrenal fatigue would become easy.

Limit Refined Salt Intake: It is another measure that can help you in addressing adrenal fatigue. There are scores of studies that tell that high salt intake leads to insulin resistance and also causes high cortisol production. It is also a significant cause of high blood pressure and dyslipidemia. The refined salt has high sodium content that can lead to all these issues. Hence, it would help if you lower your salt intake.

Limit Refined Sugar Intake: Refined sugar acts as a poison for the body. It is easy to process, and it raises your blood sugar levels instantly. It will eventually take a toll on your insulin release mechanism. Insulin resistance is the next step, where it will lead you. High sugar intake will also cause significant weight gain, cravings, and water retention in the body. All of this also has an impact on your adrenals, and you may face difficulty in sleeping. Many people experience stress and anxiety and may wake up several times a night.

Replace Refined Salt by Himalayan Salt: People have a misconception that all salts are the same. It isn't the case. The Himalayan salt is a mineral salt with only 87 percent sodium chloride content, whereas the refined table salt contains 97 to 99.9 percent sodium chloride. Himalayan salt also has more than 84 trace minerals that can help you a lot. They are highly beneficial in maintaining the electrolyte balance in the body. Although Himalayan salt is a better replacement, if you are suffering from high blood pressure, you must consult your doctor.

Exercise Regularly: It is another fantastic way to rebalance your cortisol production. Regular exercise is helpful in so many ways that you must not avoid it at any cost.

Meditate: We have already discussed the positive impact meditation can have on your mind. But, it would be additionally helpful to add that regular meditation helps in boosting the production of endorphins in your mind. They act as natural pain killers and also help in bringing down hormones that cause stress and anxiety.

Take Rest: Proper rest is crucial for the body. It helps in the healing process and also allows restoration. An empath can take up too much burden very fast, and that makes rest even more important. If you are feeling tired, there is no shame in taking a break.

Some Natural Remedies

Honey and Salt Mixture Can Help in Sleeping: As we have already discussed, sound sleep is vital for lowering stress. However, when you are already under so much anxiety and stress, restful sleep seems to evade you. Honey and Himalayan salt mixture can help you in such a case. You can mix five teaspoons of raw organic honey with a teaspoon of Himalayan salt and keep a little amount of that under your tongue. Allow some time for it to dissolve completely. This combination of salt and honey is helpful in hormone regulation, and it naturally de-stresses your body. This natural remedy is beneficial for getting deep uninterrupted sleep. You can take this concoction before going to bed every night.

Himalayan Salt Lamp: We live in a charged atmosphere. There are so many electronic devices that are continuously releasing charged positive ions in the air. Most electronic items, like mobile phones, laptops, microwave ovens, vacuum cleaners, TVs, and computers, release positive ions. If you stay indoors more, health problems like allergies, stress, and sleep deprivation can increase due to high positive ion exposure. Natural elements like lightning storms, sunlight, waterfalls, and ocean waves create negative ions. Himalayan Salt is also a natural mineral. Keeping it inside your room can help in balancing the charged atmosphere. You can place a small bulb inside a lamp made from Natural Himalayan salt. It will increase the negative ion discharge, and you'll find it easy to sleep.

Other Lifestyle Changes to Cope With Stress

Deep Breathing: We have already stressed enough on the significance of deep breathing in lowering stress. It helps in calming your nerves and settling the negative thoughts in your mind. You can practice deep breathing before going to sleep, and you'll find it easier to slip into a deep sleep. Here, it is crucial to understand that your mental state at the time of going to sleep has a significant impact on the kind of sleep you'll have. If you sleep thinking about something terrible, you are more likely to have sleep disruptions. Deep breathing helps you in driving out such thoughts, and your mind is generally very calm. It can help in having a sound sleep.

Limit Your Social Media Exposure: It might be a difficult thing to ask in the current age where people are hooked on to social media sites all the time. You may find it challenging. However, this is one step that can help you a lot in lowering stress. You may stop feeling bad about yourself, and focusing on yourself would become more manageable.

CHAPTER 8
Empaths And Relationships: Learning To Strike A Balance

The relationships are one of the most complicated aspects as far as empaths go. Empaths yearn for relationships, but they find it very hard to maintain stable relationships. Stable relationships help them recuperate from all the stress and pain in their lives, but the incorrect ones can do the opposite. In short, relationships can be the poison or the potion of empaths. It would all depend on the way an empath treats a relationship.

Some empaths struggle from the outset because they get into a relationship with the wrong person. Empaths have a powerful attraction towards narcissists and dominators. Such people are energy vampires, and they'd keep draining the empath of all the energy as well as empathy. If an empath gets into a relationship with a narcissist or a dominator, he/she would have no energy left to help anyone. These energy vampires are so strong that they begin to charge empaths negatively.

However, the bigger problem is that narcissists are not the only enemies empaths have in the matters of love and relationships. Empaths are the biggest problem by themselves. The difference in their nature and the way they treat relationships can work on its own to cause enough troubles.

This chapter would help you in understanding

- Common Reasons Due to Which Empaths Struggle in Relationships
- How Empaths Sabotage Their Relationships
- Best Ways to Strike a Balance in Relationships for More Positivity and Synergy

Common Reasons Due to Which Empaths Struggle in Relationships

For Most People, Empaths are Hard to Understand: This is the first thing that most people or the first impression they get. Empaths can sound mysterious to ordinary people, and that's not a bad thing. It is something that can be very attractive for many people, which may draw them toward empaths. But, such attractions do not last long.

Empaths have their unique struggles, and most people misunderstand them easily. They do not invest enough time and energy in knowing them properly, and that becomes a cause of the rift in relationships.

The initial charm of mystery that draws most people toward empaths becomes a cause of misunderstandings. However, the sad part is that there is very little that ordinary people can do about this. Until empaths do not become forthcoming and explain themselves and their needs to their partners, the rifts would continue.

Empaths have their unique struggles. They need more alone time, more space, more love, and more understanding due to the emotional strain they carry. But, they'll not be able to get that even from the best people in the world if they do not communicate. If you do not want to struggle in your relationships, you must learn to be open and frank with your partner. Just because you understand things without saying doesn't mean your partner would also be able to do the same. Being more open is the way empaths can have healthier relationships.

Empaths Can Sound Freaky for Many People: This is the world of expression. There are hundreds of thousands of languages that people speak across the globe. Then there are so many other ways to express what a person wants to convey. Still, the world is continually struggling with a lack of understanding. In such a world, if you somehow seem to understand most of the things your partner wants, desires, or thinks, it can freak your partner.

Everyone in this world has a few things that he doesn't want to share with anyone. There are a few things that are embarrassing, painful, and regrettable. Knowing things without telling can make people insecure as they feel threatened that their secret may be out. It can be embarrassing for most people, and they begin to avoid their empath partners.

As an empath, you must understand that communication, verbal, or non-verbal is essential. You cannot go on guessing things about your partner as that can make them freak out.

For Many People, Rapid Mood Swings Empaths have Can become Unbearable: No one likes tantrums, and that is a considerable challenge in a relationship with empaths. Empaths do not throw tantrums, but for an ordinary person, the difference between a mood swing and a tantrum may never be visible, and hence it all becomes the same for the partner.

Everyone in this world has mood swings. There is nothing wrong with having mood swings. There are days when things are not going as per your expectations, and it is usual to feel irritated and exhausted. The challenge with empaths is that the mood swings are a way of life and a regular feature in the life of an empath. An empath may begin to have mood swings due to the strong influence of people around, and that may be very hard for the partner to understand. The biggest culprit even here is a lack of communication.

If you don't want to struggle in your relationships, you must explain this aspect of your life and personality to your partner. It must not come as a surprise, all too often. Once your partner understands your position and the cause of the problem, making adjustments might become more manageable.

Empaths May Find It Hard to Live with Liers, but the World is Full of Them: It is a difficulty that every empath faces. Empaths have very high intuitive abilities. It enables them to peer deep into their partners. The partner doesn't even need to tell them anything. They would know most of the things on their own, but their partners don't understand it. It leads them to lie as usual, and that leads to relationship troubles.

It is a situation that empaths would need to learn to overcome. The deeper you try to look inside your partner, the more faults and inconsistencies you are going to find. What empaths do not understand is that they aren't looking for an ideal person for a suitable partner that has the qualities they need. As long as they keep peering inside their partners, they'll keep finding things they may not like but may not have anything to do with them. You wouldn't want to let go of a relationship over trivial things in the past, which even you may have had.

It'd be better if empaths can understand that it is the nature of people to lie about a few uncomfortable facts that we all have in our lives. The purpose of such lies is not to deceive you but to hide embarrassing things in the past. As long as that is not going to affect you, it shouldn't be a matter of concern for you. If you begin to accept people for what they are in the present and not what they have been in the past, it may become more comfortable for you to form healthier relationships.

Empaths Need Their Space, but Never Care to Explain That to Their Partners: It is again a communication problem with which most empaths struggle, but they never care to explain it to their partners.

Alone time every day or even several times a day can be the need for an empath. An empath must have some alone time to recharge. However, you cannot expect a caring partner to leave you alone when you are looking visibly upset. It can lead to significant confusion.

You want alone time to get over the feelings you are having at that moment. This alone time helps you get over your current emotions. Your partner is concerned for you and hence wants to be with you to understand you. If you demand alone time without explaining your position correctly, the partner may either begin to blame himself/ herself or misunderstand you completely, and neither of the conclusions is correct.

If you want to have a relationship built on trust and respect, you must explain your position clearly to your partner. The need for alone time is not a once in a blue moon incident; it is something that you'd need very often. There is no way it can go unnoticed. Hence, you must explain that as clearly as possible to your partner.

Empaths Dig for Toxic People: It is a weakness empaths have in general. There is a motherly attitude in all empaths that makes them big for people who need them and not the people who love them. It is a prominent reason why empaths may leave the people who love them for the people who are exploiting them.

Empaths have a weak spot for the people who need them. They want to be the saviors. It is a weakness often exploited by narcissists. They know that even if they use empaths but keep calling them back for help, they won't be able to resist coming. They understand this and exploit this weakness repeatedly.

Relationships with such people will always remain a trap. You'll keep struggling with keeping your partner happy while your partner will have the next demand ready for you. The harder you try to keep the relationship working, the more challenging it'll get, and you'll feel more burdened.

You will have to understand that as an empath, your relationships must always work in your favor and not against you. If there are relationships that have become a burden, you must cut them loose.

Choosing the wrong people for a relationship or the fear of doing so is one of the biggest reasons empaths struggle the most in their lives.

How Empaths Sabotage Their Relationships

There can be no hiding from the fact that it isn't the outside force that leads to crack in the relationships empaths have, but the destruction is of their own making. Relationships are not emotions and feelings; they are the real things. You need to work on them and nurture them. You will have to go against your impulses a few times to cater to the needs of your partner. Your partner will have to understand your needs, and you'll also need to communicate those to your partner. Empaths do not pay attention to these and remain in their world, and it becomes a cause of destruction for the relationships.

If you do not want to sabotage your relationship and want to keep it flourishing, you must take care of the following things:

Outside Your Alone Time and Your Needs, Even Your Partner Exists: The empaths are so caring and loving, yet they live in zones. There will be times when they'd not even hesitate invading the privacy of their partners, and then there would be times they'd act oblivious to their needs. These are extremes, and relationships do not work on such peaks. It is a fact that empaths need alone time and self-care. It is a fantastic thing if an empath has learned self-care and has begun devoting time to that. However, the empath would also need to be more sensitive to the needs of the partner. Your alone time must not look like exclusion or alienation to your partner. It would be best if you communicated your needs and possibly the cause. If you fail to do so, you may become the real culprit of sabotaging your relationship. You must not expect your partner to understand if you do not care to explain that to your partner.

Complications aren't Math Problems That You Can Solve in Your Head: Empaths are complicated people. They can have several things going on in their minds. They tend to think and, more often than not, overthink things. It isn't helpful in any way. However, it can be destructive for relationships.

When you keep complications in your head, your attitude changes, you might think that others might not notice, but such things are apparent. You can afford to do this once in a while, but it isn't a sustainable way to live. As an empath, you must keep repeating to yourself that communication is the key. You may not need the help of your partner in solving the problem or unloading your emotions, but not telling that to your partner will tantamount to sabotaging a relationship.

You must always be forthcoming and frank with your partner. It can be challenging at times, but it is a skill you can acquire with practice. There is no shortage of time because you are an empath for life, and hence the sooner you begin practicing it, the better.

Do not Take It as Your Right to Invade the Privacy of Your Partner: As we have already discussed, there are things that people like to keep to themselves, and you have no business invading the privacy of your partner because you are an empath.

Most empaths begin crossing this line all too often, and this can make their partners insecure. You will have to understand that like you, even your partner may like to keep a few things private, and you have no business invading the personal space of your partner.

It doesn't matter whether you do that out of concern or love; if your partner didn't tell you, there is no reason for you to tell your partner that you know it by yourself. If you do not stop and continue the invasion of the privacy of your partner, you'll sabotage the relationship you love so dearly.

Poor Communication: You may be the most understanding person on this earth and also someone the world likes, but if you do not communicate with your partner, it'll not last long.

Communication is the most important base of any relationship. When you communicate, you not only explain your problems, worries, and concerns, but you also express your trust in the other person with that information. Trust is critical, and it also forms a better understanding.

If you do not communicate appropriately with your partner, after a while, things may begin to take a toll on the relationships. For instance, if you are unable to sleep when your partner is snoring by your side, you must communicate that. People snore in their sleep. It is a condition over which people have no control. Your partner may not even know about it and hence has no-fault. But, if you do not communicate, there will be problems.

Generally, empaths are light sleepers, and hence snoring may not allow them to sleep. Lack of communication may give you sleepless nights or poor sleep. It will have an impact on your energy levels as sleep is vital for empaths. You may bear that without complaining for some time, but after a while, the feeling that the partner is uncaring may creep in. You may also begin to plan tit for tats for that.

It would help if you remembered that all this might take place while your partner may not even have proper knowledge about it or of its intensity in your life and the turmoil it may be causing.

It wasn't snoring that was the main culprit but lack of communication that led to the problem. You must have a proper mechanism to explain your needs and feelings if you do not want to sabotage your relationship.

Negligence of Self-Care: Self-care practices are vital for any empath as they help in keeping the empath empowered and compassionate. If you begin ignoring self-care practices like deep breathing, meditation, spending time in isolation, you may start to feel tired, exhausted, and irritated. Your sensitivities will take a hit, and you may begin hoarding the energies absorbed from others. To keep yourself going, you must remain light and open.

One of the most significant issues empaths face is they begin to feel ungrounded. Doubts begin encroaching their minds, and they are always fidgety. Such behavior can never be conducive to relationships.

It would help if you practiced grounding techniques, devote some time alone every day, and follow protection strategies. These will help you in staying focused and sharp.

Give Your Partner a Chance of Expressing Feelings: Empaths are gentle and caring, but they may appear intimidating in relationships because they seem to know a lot. The expression has a vital role to play in relationships. Most people know that their partners love then, but they still like to be surprised at times. They know that the partner loves them, yet listening to 'I love you' from the partner sounds sweeter than honey and embalms the heart.

However, this is an area in which empaths perform the worst. Most empaths can understand their partners and their feelings without being said. But, that doesn't mean that they can snatch the right of the partner for expressing them. There is another problem that may arise, and that is the problem caused by assumptions. What most empaths absorb are feelings. There are no clear communications. There can be times when the empath may fail to clearly understand what the partner is thinking and assume something different. Such things can complicate relationships beyond repair, and empaths may stay away from such practices.

As an empath, you have a gift that you can understand the feelings and emotions of your partner clearly. However, it would be best if you did not overuse this power to eliminate the need for communication from your partner.

Best Ways to Strike a Balance in Relationships for More Positivity and Synergy

Communicate Your Need for Physical Space: This is a thing of significance in the life of an empath. Empaths can absorb energy and feelings from people around them even when they cross them on the path. Physical contact can send strong signals, and they may soak more than they'd like to do otherwise. These are aspects of the life of an empath that other people would struggle to understand. Yet, they are undeniable facts, and ignoring them can be challenging for an empath.

However, you shouldn't expect your partner to understand these things without expressing them. Many empaths may not feel comfortable with too much physical contact. Usually, couples like to hold each other, sleep in each other's arms, and may also want to maintain physical contact more often. It may not be the case with empaths, as many empaths can feel an energy drain with too much physical connection. Although the empath may want to enjoy the company of the partner, physical contact may be all too overwhelming. It can also be the case in other areas like physical contact while sleeping or meeting.

If you feel uncomfortable with excessive physical contact, you must express that to your partner. Please do not keep it within yourself for your partner to understand. You must know that excessive bodily contact is the norm and not otherwise.

No Harm in Discussing Sleeping Arrangements: This point is also related to the discussion above. Some empaths may find physical contact overwhelming. Physical contact may be acceptable while getting intimate or lovemaking, it may not work well while they are trying to sleep.

Physical contact of another person may interfere with the energy field of others, and hence the empath may not be able to enjoy that. Some empath may wake up even just by the touch of another person. At the same time, others may face difficulties even in going to sleep. It has nothing to do with love and affection, as it is just a matter of energy.

You must discuss this with your partner in detail and make suitable arrangements. Sleep is vital for your smooth functioning, and hence it can't be ignored. At the same time, the happiness, satisfaction, and consent of your partner are also equally important, and you shouldn't forget that.

Deal with Emotions, One at a Time: Many empaths can have a lot running inside their head at the same time, and it can make their thinking cloudy. It can be very harmful as this can render the empath less productive. It also has a profound impact on the relationships, and the empath may remain lost in the thoughts and may not be able to communicate correctly.

It is something empaths must handle at the earliest. As an empath, you are emotionally sensitive. You may also pick various emotions from others, and it can overwhelm you. However, you cannot remain engaged with your thoughts all the time without a process.

It would help if you learned to deal with the biggest problem in your mind first and then touch the other ones, and in this way, you'll be able to solve most of them and even have time for your partner.

Communicate Things That Cause Discomfort: Most empaths are highly sensitive to bright lights, sounds, and other such things that can stimulate their system. Any violence or shouting would always come at the top of this ladder. While a little yelling now and then maybe a norm for many couples, it may not work for empaths. Yelling, shouting, or sudden action can overstimulate empaths, and they may not react well to them.

Your partner is not a Machine That You Can Repair: Most empaths have a savior instinct in them. It means that they want to help everyone they can and fix things. It is a habit that is difficult to control in empaths. However, it may not go down well with their partners.

Empaths absorb feelings and emotions from others. Physical empaths can also absorb energies from others and heal people. But, all of this has a cost. It overwhelms their system, and they may feel exhausted and drained. They may also become more reclusive and begin to expect a lot from their partners without putting in their contributions at all. It can be devastating for relationships.

Such expectations can lead to constant bickerings and misunderstandings. Their partners may begin to feel trapped. For the betterment of the relationship, empaths should understand the need for space for their partners. They must also have a better differentiation between the way they can behave with others and their partners. Expecting too much without contributing even a little can also be devastating for relationships, and empaths must avoid that.

Be Vocal About Your Specific Needs: Besides everything else, empaths are different, and they must not hide that from their partners. While other couples may like spooning while they sleep, empaths may even have disturbed sleep even by a simple touch of the hand. Noise is another issue that most empaths face. If their partner snores at night, empaths may have a hard time sleeping or will have disrupted sleep. It is essential to communicate these issues to your partner because these aren't the things that may go away in a few days, and you are most likely to remain that way.

If you do not communicate your discomfort from your partner, you will continue facing these issues, and only your exasperation will grow stronger. These are little things that you can adjust with your partner, and only a little understanding will do the job. However, ignoring these can be very painful for you and eventually for your partner, and hence you must do yourself and your partner a favor and explain such things as they come along your way.

As far as discussing discomfort goes, some empaths do well in that area, but most fail when it comes to explaining the things you like. If you want to do something or prefer something in your life over others, you should discuss even that with your partner.

For instance, most empaths have a love for water and baths. It is revitalizing, and it is calming and soothing. It also helps you wash down your thoughts. Therefore, they want to spend their sweet time in the baths. It can look strange or uncanny to your partner, and hence you must also be open about the things you like more than others.

Empaths must understand that relationships are all about communication and expression. They can't run them unilaterally by assuming the things their partners want or by doing things their way.

Every empath has a unique struggle, and it takes a lot of understanding, courage, and time to understand those struggles. However, before anyone else can understand those struggles, the empath may identify them with great clarity. Strangely, many empaths do not even have a clear idea of things that are troublesome for them and the things that aren't. They are just facing every moment bluntly, and that cannot be a delightful way to live.

Fixing the problems in relationships can help empaths sort one part of their life, and they'll have one corner to find support whenever they need it. Relationships are very comforting and energizing, and most empaths know that. However, most of them are unable to sustain them because they never try to understand the problems in the way and hence fail to find a solution for them.

If you follow these simple steps, you'll be able to handle your relationship troubles easily.

CHAPTER 9
It Is Common For Empaths To Feel Exhausted- Understand The Signs That Your Soul Needs Healing

Feelings of exhaustion are not uncommon for empaths. However, that doesn't mean an empath can ignore them. The feeling of exhaustion, fatigue, or tiredness can be a vital sign that you are getting overwhelmed, and your soul needs healing.

An energetic soul full of compassion and sensitivities is what makes an empath functional. If the empath begins to feel lethargic and unenthusiastic, it can be a problem for the society at large.

However, the main problem is the identification of the problem. While physical exhaustion is evident and easy to spot, the same may not be the case with the weariness of the soul. You will have to remain observant of the signs and seek healing without delay.

Healing is essential because it frees you up. You don't feel stuck in one place, and your energy flow remains smooth. An empath with an exhausted soul will neither be able to feel empowered nor stay stable and confident. If you want to seek awakening and gain a connection with the larger consciousness, you must have a healed soul.

Signs That Your Soul Needs Healing

You have Become Even More Sensitive

Being sensitive is nothing new for an empath. Hence, at the outset, this may not look like a sign. But, you may be wrong there. We all consume salt, and eating food without salt can be very tough. It adds an essential taste to the food. If the food has salt as per taste, you may not even think about it and focus on the other parts of the food. I wonder if anyone has ever complimented any chef over the balance of salt in the food. Yet, if the salt is even a little more in the food, it'll be the first thing that you'll notice. It is something you can't miss sensing in the food. If it is too much, eating food would become impossible and even harmful.

The same is the case with sensitivities. If ordinary people are sensing things with a 1x vision, you are already sensing them on 5x, and with your sensitivities inflamed, they can be at 10x or 20x. You might begin to perceive things that are not even important, or sphere of influence may start to expand.

If anything of this sort happens, you must become cautious as that can be a sign that your soul is exhausted and needs healing.

Most people would argue that when the soul is exhausted, the sensitivities should get low, and you may stop picking emotions from others, but they are incorrect. As your soul begins to get more and more burdened, your sensitivities increase, and you may feel some discomfort in your functioning.

You Have Begun Picking Emotions Randomly

It is also an extension of the previous point. When your sensitivities are high, your ability to pick emotions doesn't remain limited to a particular group. It becomes random, and you may begin facing problems in discerning, which emotion belongs to whom. It isn't a minor issue as it can lead to more exhaustion, and you may feel overburdened.

A clear distinction between your emotions and the emotions picked from others is crucial. However, when your soul is exhausted, there is no such distinction possible, and hence you may not be able to function. You simply feel tied down to such emotions.

It is a condition every empath detests because then the empath would begin to feel as bad as the people who have loaned those emotions. Those people are in a better situation because they only have one set of emotions, but you, as an empath, would have plenty of them, and hence you will begin to feel overburdened and exhausted.

If you go out and begin to feel hopelessly exhausted and miserable, it is a clear sign that your soul is getting exhausted and needs healing.

You are Mirroring Emotions of Others

An empath may experience a part of the sorrow or pain of the people from whom he/she picks up the emotions and gives a portion of positive energy to them. It is a simple exchange that enables empaths in helping others.

However, once the soul of an empath is exhausted, it isn't in a position to heal others, and the empath may begin to experience the exact emotions as others.

It means that while in ordinary conditions, you may be able to show empathy to the people you meet and help them, you will not be able to do that. Instead, you will begin mirroring their emotions and experiencing them as your own.

These experiences can be harrowing because you cannot have control over the things others feel or the situation they are in at that moment.

Besides, you will also not be in a position to help them or heal them because your soul will need healing. It is a state of utter helplessness that you wouldn't want.

You are No Longer Moving Forward

It is another impediment on the path of personal transformation that you may encounter. The purpose of life is to move ahead. As an empath, you are always moving on the path of awakening and consciousness, but an exhausted soul will not take you anywhere. You may feel stuck and confused and will have no answers for your current state.

No matter what you try to do, you'll remain confused with no clear path ahead. It is a common problem most empaths experience, and the faster you get out of it, the better because you are not going to get anywhere with this feeling.

CHAPTER 10: SELF-CARE TIPS FOR HEALING EXHAUSTION

Self-care is of paramount importance for empaths. There are no remedies for healing empaths because it isn't a disease, but a state of consciousness.

Although being an empath is not a disease or a problem, it is a condition, and there can always be better ways to cope with the blocks and impediments faced in it.

It is crucial to note that empaths have a heightened state of consciousness, and hence you'd need to be alert about the things that may cause disruption. Empaths may not feel physical barriers around them, but they may feel tied down by energy barriers.

Focus and concentration may be lacking in many empaths, and that can also pose a big problem.

Therefore, it becomes pertinent that empaths lay great emphasis on self-care and avoid exhaustion of the soul.

There are some simple practices and lifestyle modifications that can significantly help an empath deal with exhaustion. Most of the things are easy to deal with, and you'd not find any difficulty in assimilating these steps in your life.

Meditate

There is no better advice for empaths that can be more helpful for them. Meditation opens the windows of calm and deep relaxation for empaths. It is also a fantastic way to get over the emotional overload. No matter how heavy and unsettled you may be feeling, you will be able to get over those feelings with the help of meditation.

Whether you are feeling ungrounded, confused, overwhelmed, or anxious, meditation is the answer to all these problems. Most meditation sessions don't need any special preparation, and you can do them at any peaceful place.

If you are unable to sleep at night or even feel lethargic in the morning, meditation will help you immensely.

Inculcate a Hobby

More than anything else, empaths suffer from the malice of overthinking. They are living in their minds, and hence thinking comes naturally and turns into overthinking.

However, this doesn't bring clarity but creates clutter. Empaths become more confused and fearful than they already were. It is a problem that can quickly turn nasty.

The best way to get out of the trap of this problem is to engage yourself in some hobby. You can select anything that you like but prevent too much idle time where you can contemplate on useless things.

Having a productive hobby has many positive aspects, and one of them is confidence building. The more you do something that you love, the more positive you'll feel about yourself.

Give the Internet or Social Media a Miss, Whenever You Can

Although this is helpful advice for everyone in general, it is incredibly beneficial for empaths, in particular. Excessive social media exposure can fill you with toxic feelings that may be harmful to empathy.

When we are looking at the make-believe world of social media, we tend to get swayed. However, we know that most of the things portrayed on social media platforms are not as they look. Most of it is a façade. People looking incredibly happy and fortunate on these platforms are hiding behind several filters. Yet it fills us with remorse.

Our mind likes to believe in those pictures and then feel sad. It isn't something that can lead to positive energy build-up. That's why you must try to maintain a safe distance from the internet, especially the social media sites that only lead to wastage of time and accumulation of negative energy.

Learn the Art of Time Management

Nobody needs more rest and breaks than an empath. It is a necessity for an empath but may be hard to obtain in this highly competitive world. Therefore, you do not have an option but to devise innovative ways to find those short breaks to rest.

Everything else must remain secondary to you in front of rest because you are more likely to feel exhausted as compared to your friend, who takes frequent coffee breaks to chit-chat with others.

Therefore, you should focus on finishing your work faster and finding time to relax.

Set Healthy Personal Boundaries

Lack of personal boundaries is a problem most empaths face. Empaths are naturally absorbing feelings, emotions, and energies from the people around them. If they do not have healthy personal boundaries, this can intensify, and they may begin picking feelings and emotions left, right, and center.

For their wellbeing, they must have healthy personal boundaries. They must know the way to maintain a safe distance from people and not allow everyone within their comfort zone.

They also must devise ways to form a protective energy shield around them that can prevent the seepage of emotions very quickly.

Spend Time With Nature

Nature is the best place for an empath to be. Nature can rejuvenate an empath. You may feel energized and healed in the presence of nature.
Nature contains negative ions, and that can balance the presence of positive ions accumulated by you.
The greenery, plants, trees, mountains, and oceans can absorb all the negativity, feelings, and emotions held by them.
There is no better place to heal for an empath than the lap of nature.
If you are feeling too overwhelmed by emotions, you can hug a tree, and you will feel lighter, and the tress can absorb your emotions.

Focus on Alone Time

Alone time is another primary requirement of any empath. It is time an empath needs to heal internal wounds and complications. Lack of communication and self-care can make many empaths ignore the need for alone time, but soon they'll begin feeling overwhelmed and exhausted.
If you are also feeling so, then you must also put your focus on alone time. Just sit in loneliness, and you'll find it easier to unload all the emotions that you might have absorbed over time.

Limit Your Physical Contact

Shaking hands and hugging may have become a norm, but they aren't a necessity, especially for an empath. Handshakes, hugs, and kisses make you touch the other person, and you may absorb more than you'd like to do. Most people are hiding their emotions behind their calm demeanor, but as an empath, you may pick even those emotions and feel their pain. If you do not want to feel exhausted rapidly, you must try to avoid or at least limit physical contact. For greeting others, you can use even more polite gestures like bowing your head or even folding your hands like in the Asian cultures.
The tradition of folding the hand also came from sages and seers in the eastern traditions. They also believed that the exchange of energy takes place when you touch someone, and that's why they wished everyone with folding their hands or by nodding their hands.

CHAPTER 11
Preventing Influence Of Negative Energies

Proper management of energies is of great significance for empaths. Empaths are radiating positive healing energy and absorbing negative energies. If they do not manage the influence of negative energies properly, they might start feeling exhausted rapidly.

Therefore, if you want to avoid feeling drained and exhausted frequently, you must try to prevent the influence of negative energies.

Protection of your energy field may seem to be a very tough task as your exposure to various kinds of energy influences is high, but it is an actionable job.

In this chapter, we will try to learn various ways to prevent the influence of negative energies.

Before we move ahead, you must understand that we get negative energy or what we call negative vibes from people around us. Some people are full of positive energy, and when you go near them, you feel positive, pleasant, confident, and radiant. You'll have all these feelings within you instantly. However, the same person can also radiate negative energy with feelings of anger, contempt, and aggression, depending on the current state of mind. It is essential to understand that energy or life-force is never static. It is always changing form.

The same person can give you positive vibes in a specific state of mind and radiate negative vibes in others. Therefore, you must not be judgemental about others or have prejudices.

There will be people who would have an extremely negative energy sphere, and when you go near them, you might feel a burden upon you. It is always better to avoid going around such people, if possible.

Essential Tips to Prevent Negative Energy Influence

Be Cautious and Maintain Distance: One of the most significant advantages of being an empath is that you can sense energies far better than others. It is a boon that most empaths don't appreciate.

Consider yourself going near the same person without knowing the negative influence that person can have on you. The energy or vibes people radiate are reflective of their personality and temperament. If a person is radiating negative vibes even while talking as if dropping honey drops, you can understand the damage that person could have caused.

You should always use this gift to your advantage and stay away from people who are radiating negative vibes. If avoiding such people altogether is not possible, you must maintain at least a distance of a few feet. Please do not be ashamed of keeping a safe space between you and that person because it is going to have a profound impact on you.

Maintain Boundaries: As an empath, very few things would be as helpful as having boundaries. Most empaths feel that they are unable to create boundaries. These boundaries are not physical but energy boundaries. You can firm boundaries if you can follow detachment. The more you get identified with someone or something, the harder it will get to prevent it from intruding on your energy field.

Many people misunderstand detachment as disassociation. There is a significant difference between both. Detachment means that you do not get affected by everything or anything happening to that thing or person. In that case, the negative influence of such people goes down.

Deep Breathing and Meditation: Deep breathing is a beneficial technique when you feel you are getting overwhelmed by the negative influence of people around you. It helps you calm your mind, and the process of absorbing negative energy would also slow down. You do not need any special preparation for deep breathing. You can also regulate your breathing while you are standing alongside the person, influencing you negatively.

In case the negative influence is very high, and you feel that deep breathing isn't helping much, you can also do meditation to calm your senses. Meditation is a powerful technique to overcome the influence of negative energies. It gives you complete control of your body and your mind, and you can quickly cleanse all the negative energy.

Perceive a Protective Shield Around You: It is a fantastic technique that you can use when you are in certain areas where you find it difficult to avoid the influence of negative energy. For instance, if you are sitting in the waiting room of a clinic or hospital surrounded by people suffering from various ailments, it is easy to get influenced by negative energy in such circumstances.

In such cases, you can imagine a protective shield around you and command it to protect you. Many people may feel that it wouldn't work, but that's not the case. Like you can get influenced by negative energies around you, there is also a positive energy shield within you. When at such places, imagine a white protective bubble forming around you. Your aura can prevent negative energies from influencing you.

Stop Reacting to People and Their Provocations: There will be people around you who might try to provoke and enrage you. Reacting to such people will lead to rage and contempt. Your positive energy shield will weaken, and the influence of negative energy would increase. You should avoid reacting to such people as their provocations.

Do not Pay Heed to the Opinion of Others About You: We continuously strive to become more acceptable and have higher approval of people around us. It is neither needed nor a standard, yet we are not able to keep the temptation away.

You must avoid doing this. When you begin caring for the opinion of others a lot, you need to change yourself against your true nature. Not only this, but we also become more prone to criticism, and our capacity to bear negative criticism goes down. It will have a profound impact on our energy center, and it may even get repressed

You should remember that self-improvement is a continuous process that never stops and must begin from within you. Any change brought to impress someone will always remain temporary.

If you follow these simple tips, you will be able to prevent your energy shield and not get negatively influenced by others.

CHAPTER 12
Energy Cleansing

When it comes to looking after ourselves, our primary focus is always on our physical bodies. We pay attention to all the signs and symptoms of disorder arising in the physical body. However, the physical body isn't the only body that we have. Besides the physical body, we also have a spiritual body and an energy body.

Although the other two bodies do not get much mention, they are as important as our physical body. Any imbalance in the spiritual body or the chakras can lead to sluggishness, eating disorders, anxiety, fear, panic attacks, overthinking, depression, nightmares, and other such symptoms.

Our energy body or our aura is a reflection of our energies, emotions, and spirituality. We all have an aura around us. There are even procedures that can capture the aura, and it can depict our current mood and emotional state more accurately.

People ignore the energy body as it isn't visible, but it is also equally important. It is the body that gets influenced by energies around us, and ultimately it will affect our physical body too.

Most people seldom pay attention to this, but there will be times when all of a sudden, mood takes a significant drop. There is nothing to make us depressed or sad, but we still stop feeling happy. Kids may fall sick all of a sudden and then recover. All this happens when our energy body comes under a negative influence. Other energy sources around us begin influencing us, and sometimes they win.

This process of constant invasion of energy fields is even more rigorous in empaths or people trying to awaken their third eye chakra. It happens because your energy field expands, and your sensitivities are at their peak.

The people who are trying to awaken their third eye chakra are consciously trying to expand their energy fields and sensitivities, and therefore they are more cautious. They take elaborate steps to protect their energy field so that there is no invasion. But empaths have that on default mode, and that's why they can get careless about protecting and cleansing their energies.

In this chapter, we will try to understand various ways to cleanse your energy so that you don't come under the influence of negative energies trying to invade your body.

Balancing Your Chakras

Chakras are energy centers in our body that dominate the endocrine glands. They control and manage the flow of energy inside and outside our bodies. We have seven energy centers virtually located along our spinal cord, and they play a crucial role in the flow of energy, emotions, and abilities.

How our energies would interact and perform against the energies trying to invade our body would depend on the energy balance in the chakras and their performance.

These chakras can get blocked, obstructed, and closed due to various reasons. If your chakras are out of balance or inactive, you may become susceptible to the negative influence of energies.

You can practice simple chakra balancing meditations once a day to keep the chakras aligned. It will help you immensely in preventing the negative influence of energy.

Smudging

All sorts of energies are all around us. People and various other life forms have lived for millions of years before us, and those energies try to influence us all the time.

When you are very positive, your energy field is strong, but it attracts a lot of negative energy towards itself. These energies can also have a strong presence and influence, even in your home.

If you do not cleanse your home and yourself of these energies, you may begin to feel tied down and heavy.

Smudging is an easy way to cleanse the influence of negative energies. If you are feeling out of sync, you can take white sage and smudge your energy field as well as your house with it, and you'll feel lighter.

You can even smudge your house regularly with white sage to get a positive feeling and remain protected.

Creation of Sacred Space

It is another way to keep yourself protected and give yourself a chance to breathe freely without fear of the influence of negative energies. You can designate any place or corner in your home or office as your sacred space and prohibit entry of anyone else to that part. You can use this place for meditation, and you'll find that building focus would be much more comfortable in this corner. If you are feeling exhausted or anxious, this corner will provide the required relief.

You do not need to do anything specific to this space. You can go and meditate at that place regularly, and that would be enough. Such sites retain your positive energy and the energy from the meditation and keep getting more potent in their positive energy fields.

If you have such a place designated in your home or office, you'll find it easy to focus and deal with your vulnerable state.

Wash Your Hands with LukeWarm Water

It is another technique that can help you in cleaning your energy field. When you feel that you are feeling low or sad, you can wash your hands with soap and lukewarm water.

It will cleanse your energy field, and you'll feel better.

External and Internal Water Cleansing

External Cleansing: Water is a fantastic energy cleanser. If you are feeling stressed, anxious, or feeling confused, merely standing under the shower for a few minutes can help you a lot.

When the water runs over your body from head to toe, it not only rinses your body but also cleans your energy field. You can try it whenever you are feeling tied down.

Internal Cleansing: You can undertake internal cleansing by drinking water very mindfully. Do not merely drink water, but through your awareness, also try to follow its path inside the body. Visualize your body getting cleansed as the water goes down. It will help you feel better.

Epsom Salt Baths with Essential Oils

Epsom salt is beneficial in clearing the influence of negative energies. You can mix some Epsom salt or any other sea salt in your bathtub or rub it in your hands while you apply soap on your body, and it will help you in cleansing your energy field.

Epsom salt has tremendous importance in cleansing the energy fields, and hence it can be used in various ways.

You can also add a few drops of essential oils in the water, and that would also help you in calming down and clearing the negative energies.

Removing Blockages through Reiki

Reiki is a fantastic energy healing technique. It also works on the principles of energy fields in the body, like the chakras. You can take the help of Reiki healers in unblocking your energy centers, and it can also help you in getting rid of several physical ailments caused by such blockages.

Use Crystals and Protective Stones

Humankind has been using crystals since time immemorial. Our ancestors used them even when they had no scientific way of knowing their constitution and properties. Now that we have all the resources and knowledge of science by our side, we know that crystals have an excellent balance of minerals that can soak specific energies.

Crystals can help us clear various energy influences. They open the doors of spiritual awakening.

Some helpful crystals are:

Agate: It can enhance your focus and help in meditation. If you feel unsettled, you can wear this crystal to bring inner peace, and it will also help in getting your thoughts and spirit in harmony.

Amethyst: This crystal is helpful in spiritual healing. It is the protector. It prevents you from psychic attacks and negative energies. It also enhances your psychic gifts and the power of intuition.

Aquamarine: It gives you the gift of sharp vision and intuition. It protects you from negative energies.

Calcite: It cleans your energy field and amplifies it. It balances the chakras and improves your psychic abilities.

Jade: It is a protector crystal. It also helps in finding your spiritual path.

Kunzite: This crystal helps you in meditation and also prevents you from the influence of negative energies. It helps in healing too. It aligns your heart chakra.

Black Tourmaline: This is an excellent stone you can use for grounding your spirit. This stone is electrical vibrations and helps you in establishing a connection with mother earth. It aligns your energy with the energy of the planet.

Black Obsidian: As far as protection from negative energies is concerned, this crystal works excellent. It can absorb all the negative energy around you, providing excellent protection.

CHAPTER 13
GROUNDING TECHNIQUES FOR EMPATHS

Most empaths act as emotional sponges. They keep absorbing feelings and emotions of people around them and also various kinds of energies that might not always be positive and conducive. All this can overwhelm the empath and overstimulate the system.

Awakened empaths are better at managing the emotions they pick, and they can also stop absorbing the feelings and emotions when they feel overwhelmed. However, not all empaths are capable of doing this, and it can make them feel exhausted and drained very quickly.

If the empath has absorbed too much and the system gets overstimulated, it can make them feel ungrounded and unsettled. It can cause anxiety, frustration, and doubt.

Grounding techniques are beneficial in making them feel more sensitive, settled, and focused. You can practice most of these grounding techniques anytime you begin to feel disconnected. There are some measures like wearing gemstones that help in remaining protected, and you can prevent overstimulation easily. There are other grounding techniques like meditation that you can practice anytime you feel out of touch with your faculties.

Walking barefoot on the ground and taking a bath are also a few grounding techniques that can be helpful.

We will now discuss these grounding techniques in detail.

Water
Water is a fantastic element that can help you feel grounded immediately. If you are feeling overwhelmed, overstimulated, or agitated, you can take a warm water bath, and you'll feel calm and grounded. Water can rinse off the negative energy, and it calms your nerves. While you are taking a shower or soaking in the bathtub, you must remain mindful of the effect of water on your body.

Water is a natural element that is very powerful and has the tendency to run towards the ground. It quickly connects you with the earth, and you will feel more safe and secure.

If it's raining, you can even soak in the rain as it is natural water dripping from the sky. The drops falling from the sky help your senses in waking up.

If you feel that you have a charged atmosphere at your home, you can also place a miniature fountain in your home as décor. It will not only beautify your place but also make you feel more grounded.

People living near water bodies can also go near the water body to feel more grounded.

Use of Oil and Incense to Feel Grounded

Oils, fragrances, and incenses have played a significant role historically. They are used in most spiritual processes because they can calm your nerves and make you focused. Most oils, fragrances, and incenses are natural, and hence they can assimilate with your senses quickly without causing any overpowering impact.

Our ancestors have been using them since time immemorial for various spiritual processes. Native Americans still use natural herbs and fragrances like white sage, cedar, juniper, sweetgrass, and pine needles for cleaning areas of all the negative energy.

Natural incenses can calm your nerves, and you can quickly feel grounded. White sage is also used for cleansing crystals of their negative energies that they might have retained from their previous owners.

You can also use essential oils in the bath or directly on your skin mixed with some carrier oil. You must be careful while using essential oils on your skin as some people may be allergic to some essential oils due to their robust nature.

You can also use essential oils in diffusers and humidifiers for a more energetic environment and better grounding effect.

The use of essential oils in diffusers and humidifiers also helps in healthy sleep, relieving headaches, and alleviating pain.

Meditation

Meditation plays a very significant role in calming you down and grounding you to the earth. When you meditate, you consciously correct the flow of energy in your body.

Meditation connects you to the roots, and the energy in your body can pass to the ground. The earth absorbs all the negative energy inside you and fills you with warm energy. You can also practice specific grounding meditation or root chakra meditation for a better grounding effect.

When you meditate, the unfiltered raw emotions inside you seep into the ground, and you get the warm sensation that settles you ultimately.

You can practice the following meditation for better grounding effect:

Sit in a comfortable posture

If possible, sit with your legs crossed.

If you are uncomfortable, sit in any comfortable posture on the ground

Keep your back upright

Do not slouch as that will obstruct the flow of energy and you may even begin to feel lethargic

Close your eyes gently

Breathe in

Breathe out

Let your breathing rate come to a natural pace

Do not try to force your breathing

Allow it to become natural on its own

Breathe in

Breathe out
At the base of your spine is the root chakra
It is your connection to the mother earth
It draws its energy from the ground
It will help you connect deeply
You do not need to do anything
There is no need to think anything
You are in a safe space
Mother earth will nurture you with its soothing energy
Take a deep breath through your nose
Do it slowly
Do not rush
Just keep breathing the rejuvenating air
As the air fills up your belly
Observe that air through your awareness
It will fill your body with light
As it fills your gut
It will seep into every part of your body
The fresh air will mix in your body
It will expel the spent air out through every part of your body
Now exhale very slowly through your mouth
Do not rush the process
Exhale slowly
Push out all the air inside your gut
Relax
Breathe in
Breathe out
Now take your awareness to your root chakra
Right at the base of your spine
The part that's touching the ground
Now, visualize the red energy at the base of your spine
It is the energy at your root chakra
It will absorb all the negativity inside you
Visualize that red spot expanding slowly
It will get more significant as it absorbs all the negativity inside you
Feel that energy seeping into the ground
Feel the ground under you getting warm
It is the mother earth radiating its soothing warm energy
Your root chakra will absorb this energy and re-energize you
You will feel calm prevailing over you
All doubts will begin to melt as you receive more positive energy
Breathe in
Breathe out
As you inhale and exhale
Feel that ball of energy rising and spreading out in your body

It is making you feel lighter and calmer
Keep breathing calmly
Let your breathing return to normal
You can now open your eyes gently and feel grounded and healed
All your doubts will have melted
You can now open your eyes.

Crystals

Crystals and gemstones can also play a very crucial role in keeping you grounded. You can wear crystals as ornaments so that they remain in contact with your body and keep you centered and grounded.

You can also keep gems in a pouch and keep them on your person all the time when you go out, and they'll help in thwarting negative energies and would also keep your calm.

You only need to be cautious while procuring gemstones. Some gemstones can be very costly, and people wear their cheap artificial alternates. That doesn't work that well because the gems need to be natural to give their best effects. In place of using the synthetic varieties, you can use the cheaper but natural alternatives, and they can also have a similar impact.

Spend Time in the Lap of Nature

Nothing can calm your senses like nature, and it also has a fantastic grounding effect. If you are feeling very unsettled and depressed and your soul needs healing and grounding, you can go to any park full of trees, lakes, rivers, mountains, or a beach. All these natural surroundings have a significant grounding effect. They are very absorbing and would soak all the stress and negative energy stored inside you.

Try to spend more time in such locations very often as they can help you with your healing process as well as allow grounding.

Do not go to such places with anyone else as that can cause a disturbance, and you'd need a lot of alone time. If you are with some people, try to find someplace where there aren't too many people so that you can be with nature in peace.

Water bodies are especially helpful as they are very absorbing, and you can quickly establish a connection with them.

Walk Barefoot

It is another way to feel grounded quickly. You can walk on the green grass barefoot in the morning when it still holds the dew drops. Walking on such grass calms your senses completely.

If you have woken up with lethargy and you are not feeling like doing anything, walking barefoot on the dew drops can have a magical effect on your mood as well as your energy levels.

Take off your shoes on the grass and walk for a few minutes on the grass leisurely.

If you begin to feel shaken, confused, agitated, and frustrated in the day, walking barefoot on the ground will still help you in calming your senses.

You can follow these grounding techniques anytime, and they always have a very soothing impact. You will feel more at peace and will be able to focus better on the task at hand.

CHAPTER 14
Guided Meditations For Empaths

Keeping the mind calm and having full control of the senses is of paramount importance for an empath. These aren't the skill sets that all empaths will have that easily. It will take some effort, practice, and realization to become calm and aware.

Even awakened empaths can begin to feel overwhelmed at times and may need an outlet to release the acquired feelings and emotions.

Guided meditations are beneficial in this. You can record the following guided meditations in your voice and listen to them every night and meditate, or you can even listen to them whenever you feel overstimulated and ungrounded.

Guided Meditation to Calm the Mind and Release Overload of Emotions

It is always effortless to build focus if you meditate at the same place because that place would retain your positive energy. If you are away, even then, you can do this meditation, and it would have the same positive impact.

For doing meditation, it is always best to be as comfortable as possible. If you can change, then wear loose-fitting clothes for meditation. If that's not possible, at that moment, then try to loosen your clothes to be more comfortable.

Please wash your hands and feet as that would help in cleansing the negative emotions.

Sit in a comfortable position
Keep your spine upright
While you meditate, you must remain mindful that you don't slouch
You can use a backrest if you need
Please keep your neck upright
Do not use a neck rest for support as that can make you feel drowsy
Keep your shoulders straight
But, do not make them stiff
Now, close your eyes gently
Do not squeeze them
You do not need to block the light
Closing the eyes helps only in centering your awareness
Now, relax for completely
Just breathe lightly
You do not need to force your breath at the moment
Let it retain its natural pace
Breathe in

Breathe out
Breathe in
Breathe out
Let the air go in
Allow it to go out unobstructed
At this moment
Do not think about anything
It is not the time to think
It is time to be aware
Become aware of everything around you
Try to feel the sensation of the air on your skin
Feel your clothes as the places they come in contact with your skin
Become aware of the sensation
Try to feel the fragrance in the air
Does it feel sweet
Can you identify the smell
Become aware of that smell
Try to listen to the faintest noises around you
The whirring of the fan
The noise coming from the air conditioning
Try to visualize the light in front of your closed eyes
Do you see a source of light through your awareness
Try to identify the color of the light in front of your eyes
Bring your awareness to your breathing
Become mindful of the process of breathing
It is such a magnificent process
Breath coming in and going out
It is a continuous process
We are always unaware of the beauty of the process
Feel it with your senses.
Your breathing has stabilized now
It has regained its natural pace
There are no rapid breaths
Now, we will do deep breathing
You'll keep your awareness tied to your breath
Remain aware of every breath you take
Follow the path the breath takes through your awareness
With your eyes closed, you'll be able to see things that aren't visible with your eyes open
You can see far beyond the visual range with your eyes closed
Breathe in through your nose
Breathe out through your mouth
Do not try to rush the process
Be as delicate as you can be
Continue inhaling air to the count of 5

Hold the breath for another 5 seconds
Finally, continue releasing the breath to the full count of 7
Longer exhalations will help you relax
You'll feel calmer and centered
Begin inhaling fresh air
1
Feel the freshness of the air coming in
2
Does the air feel cold or warm?
3
Feel the sensation of the air around the point of entry at your nostrils
4
Feel its fragrance
5
Follow it through your awareness entering your body
1
Now hold the air
2
It would help if you remained still
3
Allow the pressure to build
4
There is no need to feel alarmed
5
Let the pressure mount
1
Now begin releasing the air slowly through your mouth
2
Do not rush the process
3
Push all the air stored in the body out
4
Put your belly towards your back as you exhale
5
Keep exhaling a little longer
6
Push out all the air within you
7
Let the last drop of air exit
Relax!
Feel the ease and comfort in your body
Deep breathing helps in cleaning the system and taking off the mind from the concerns bothering it
It is a relaxing process
Again begin inhaling through your nose

1
Now visualize the air as a white light entering your body
2
Feel its glow at the point of entry
3
Watch it illuminate your body
4
Follow the inflating your chest as it fills your lungs
5
Visualizing it going inside and filling your gut
1
Now hold this illuminate air in your body
2
Allow it to soak all the darkness and negativity stored inside
3
Allow it the time to mix with your blood and reach every cell
4
Feel the white light in your gut getting darker as the fresh air goes in and the spent air comes out
5
Feel the pressure on your lungs
1
Now release the air very slowly through your mouth with your lips forming a circle and making a sound
2
Let all the negativity come out of the body
3
With this spent air, all the exhaustion and fatigue would also come out
4
Push out everything that has been bothering you
5
Do not fear anything; you are in control
6
Push out more air so that there is space for the fresh air
7
Give a final push to the spent air
Relax!
Doesn't it feel great!
Breathe in
Breathe out
Allow your breathing to return to normal
You do not need to control your breathing anymore
You need to relax completely
Feel the calm taking over your body
Inhale

Exhale
Visualize the process through your awareness
Now focus your awareness at the center of your eyebrows
Visualize a light at that point
As you focus your awareness
You'll see that source of light expanding
Your awareness has no limits
It is as vast as this universe and ever-expanding
Keep your focus glued to that light
As you focus the light would keep expanding and coming near your point of awareness
This massive bowl of light is your awareness
It is limitless
You can enter it
Do not hesitate
Step into it, and you'll find ultimate calm
Take a step into it
You are light as a feather
You'll not fall
Visualize the white light all around you
It is the soothing light of your awareness
It is spotless
Move ahead
Do not hesitate
As you move ahead, you feel sand under your feet
The fog has settled around you
You can see a sandy beach of a mountain lake
The sight of clear blue water fills you with pleasantness and joy
There is a mountain on the other side
There are trees behind your back
And there is this blue lake flowing in front of you
The sunlight is getting reflected on its surface
There is calm all around
There is not a soul besides you here
It is the peace and calm you have been looking for
Rejoice in this calm and heal
Move closer to the shore
The water is looking tempting
You haven't touched it yet, but it is calming your soul
 Go near it
At your back you see tall trees inviting you
They are your shield from the rush of the world
They will provide you the refuge you need
A gust of wind touches your face
You feel the cold waft

The water seems to be cold
There is no other way to know if it is cold than to feel it on your feet
You want to swim in these clear waters
You are concerned about the cold
But, maybe the water is not as cold as you think it is
There is no better way than to touch it
You still resist the temptation
Sit down on the sand
It is as calming as the water
Look at the lake
See how calm it looks
It seems as if nothing is happening inside it
But, underneath, there is a lot of activity
Just like your heart
There is so much inside you
But, you are calm
You and the lake are similar
You can take the calm of the lake and transfer some of your burden to it
The lake is vast
It can take all that you have to give
Do not hesitate to pour your heart into the lake
The water is touching your feet
It is cold but not chilly
Now you have made up your mind
You want to swim in this lake
You begin to take off your shirt
You have the swimwear underneath
There is nothing that can stop you from swimming
The water on the shore is washing your feet
It is inviting you inside the lake
You feel more than ready to go inside
You move a little further
Now your ankles are underwater
The water is softly splashing on your feet
All your anxiety, anguish, anger, and sorrow has begun to precipitate
All the emotions are settling down, and the calm and cold of the water is filling you
You go a little further
Now you are standing in knee-deep water
You can feel the water filling you completely
It is time to take a dip
Feel the calm as the water comes over your head
It has the power to settle any negativity
There is no place for negative energy now
Let the calm of the lake prevail over you

Take a swim in the lake
Feel the cold water calm your nerves completely
You've never enjoyed swimming like this
There is no agitation or anguish left
You are floating on the water without an effort
You are as light as a feather now
You are feeling more confident now
You want to explore the other shore of the lake
It is an expansive lake
But you think you can cross it
There is nothing to stop you
There is no danger
There is no apprehension
You begin swimming
With every stroke
You are pushing out all the negative thoughts from your body
All the feelings and emotions that you have absorbed will get washed away as you swim in the lake
It is the cleanser you needed
You have almost reached the other shore
It is as calm as the other one
You sit in the sand to relax
As you sit in the sand, you feel your body sinking in
Mother earth is accepting in nature
It has sheltered you
It is nestling under its soft arms
You feel the gratitude
You are always absorbing the feelings and emotions of others
No one is caressing and nurturing you
You feel that care in the sand
You decide you sit in the sand for a little longer
It is comforting
You feel calm
You feel grounded
There is no chaos inside you
You only feel gratitude
The white sand is inviting you
Walk on it for a while
It feels so soft under the feel
Every step in the sand leaves an imprint
But soon the waves wash away everything
You are also the same
You absorb so many feeling and emotions
But, releasing them is also that simple
There is no need to keep anything

Like this shore
It is giving every step its imprint
But soon, it washes everything and becomes a clean slate
An empath absorbs a lot
But you do not need to keep anything inside you
You act as a sponge
You soak everything easily
But you can also clear everything with a simple squeeze
It is time to get back
You once again get back to water
You have to swim to the other shore
The journey back is even easier than before
There is nothing in your heart making you heavy
You are swimming without an effort
You have reached the other shore
You do not want to get out
The water is refreshing
You can sit on the beach for as long as you wish
Nothing is stopping you from doing what pleases you the most
There is no rush
It is your world
Look at the sun
It is setting down
It has attained the pinkish hue or is it a mixture of orange-red
There is no brightness
Just the calm red ball of light
You can see it within squinting your eyes
The sun has never looked so beautiful
It is time to get back
You wear your clothes
You look at the trees standing as a fence
Everything away from the beach is green
It fills your heart with pleasure
There are trees of all sizes on the beach
With the wind blowing lightly, they seem to dance
You begin walking back
You are feeling light now
Nothing is weighing you down
You feel light as a feather
The white light has engulfed you again
It is all calm here
You are feeling peaceful
Bring your awareness back to that source of light
Now, visualize that ball of light shrinking
It is getting back to a singularity

Take your awareness back to your breathing
Are you breathing fast?
Let your breathing return to normal
Inhale
Exhale
Inhale
Exhale
Feel your breath once again
Feel the calm entering your body with every breath
Exhale all the remaining stress with every breath
Breathe in
Breathe out
Now bring your awareness back to your body
Become aware of everything around you
Try to feel the sensation of the air on your skin
Feel your clothes as the places they come in contact with your skin
Become aware of the sensation
Try to feel the fragrance in the air
Does it feel sweet
Can you identify the smell
Become aware of that smell
Try to listen to the faintest noises around you
The whirring of the fan
The noise coming from the air conditioning
Try to visualize the light in front of your closed eyes
Do you see a source of light through your awareness
Try to identify the color of the light in front of your eyes
Bring your awareness to your breathing
Become mindful of the process of breathing
With your eyes closed
Try to move your fingers a little
Now, shake your hands
You can now open your eyes when you are ready
Do not try to stand up at once
Enjoy the calm and peace you are feeling
Remain seated for a few more moments
You can stand whenever you feel comfortable
Thank You!

CONCLUSION

Thank you for making it through to the end of this book; let's hope it was informative and able to provide you with all of the tools you need to achieve your goals, whatever they may be.

Empath healing is a fundamental concept that remains largely ignored. However, that doesn't mean it is of lesser significance. Most empaths keep struggling all their lives because they overlook the importance of protecting and healing their energy centers.

This book has tried to explain the importance of empath healing, the areas it will affect, and how you can carry out empath healing.

Most people think that healing is a complex process, and they may be unable to achieve the desired results. They are wrong, and they have never tried empath healing.

Empath healing is a combination of meditation, breathing exercises, grounding techniques, and some lifestyle changes. They are easy to follow, and the results they fetch can help you in leading a better life that isn't full of insecurities and limitations.

With the help of this book, you can incorporate these healing techniques into your life and benefit to a large extent.

Through this book, I have tried to explain every part of empath healing in detail so that you face no difficulty in applying them in your life.

This book would help you understand various ways to carry out Empath Healing.

It would give you a detailed account of all the healing strategies and how you can enforce your energy fields.

I hope that you will be able to gain full advantage of the information provided by this book.

Finally, if you enjoyed this book, please let me know your thoughts with a short review on Amazon. It means a lot, thank you!

DESCRIPTION

Learn Actionable Steps to Get Over Exhaustion and Fatigue Caused by Empath Overload

Do you feel exhausted and tired all the time?
Do you feel overstimulated and overwhelmed in crowded places?
Do you know that these can be the symptoms of empath overload?
Do you know you can overcome all these symptoms and lead a socially healthy life through empath healing?
If you want to learn the secrets of living a socially comfortable life without numbing your sensations, **Read More...**
Most people keep bearing overwhelming emotions and feel drained without knowing the root cause behind them.
They are fearful of overpowering emotions but don't know the cause
They fear crowded places but don't know how to handle them when they have to go to crowded places
They struggle with forming stable relationships all their lives but find them unable to sustain even the compatible partners
Not understanding the trials and tribulations of being an empath and the workarounds can make your life miserable.
Do you want to know the secret to deal with all these issues with ease? **Read More...**
Dealing with emotions and emotional overload is very challenging for empaths. Most empaths suffer from emotional overload due to this.
Do you know the real reason empaths feel so lonely and crave for relationships?
Do you also know the specific emotional triggers empaths face and the ways to deal with them?
Did you know that even deep breathing can be a great help in preventing emotional overload?
Did you also know the power of rhythmic breathing, controlled breathing, Pranayama, and heart chakra meditation?
Even simple breathing exercises can be of immense help in preventing emotional overload, and you can subside emotional triggers completely through heart chakra meditation.
Do you want to learn these breathing exercises and the magical heart chakra meditation? **Read More...**
Many empaths live all their life dependent on various addictions. They don't know the way out of addictions. Do you want to learn practical and actionable strategies to get out of addictions?
Poor sleep and fatigue are the biggest enemies of empaths. Yet, most empaths struggle with these issues because most of the suggested ways are not practical.

Do you want to learn about practical ways to get peaceful sleep to overcome exhaustion? **Read More…**

Striking a balance in the relationship and forming stable and productive relationships is an ongoing challenge for most empaths.

Most empaths do not pay attention to the common reasons relationships don't work out for them

They ignore the steps that can sabotage their relationships

They don't know the steps to strike a balance

Do you want to learn the ways to make your relationships work? **Read More…**

In this book, you will find:
- The miracle of empath healing and the changes it can bring in your life
- A complete understanding of the root causes behind most of the problems
- Actionable ways to deal with emotional triggers
- Practical ways to handle addictions so that there is no relapse
- Ways to deal with stress and fatigue and sleeplessness
- Key insights about the causes behind relationship troubles and ways to find a balance in relationships
- Self-care tips for dealing with exhaustion
- Ways to prevent the influence of negative energies causing a drain on you
- Practical ways of energy cleansing
- Ways to keep yourself grounded
- Guided meditation to find calm and stability

And More…..

www.ingramcontent.com/pod-product-compliance
Lightning Source LLC
Chambersburg PA
CBHW071447070526
44578CB00001B/248